THE
CHURCH LEADER'S
HANDBOOK

A Guide to Counseling Families
and Individuals in Crisis

WILLIAM R. CUTRER

Kregel
Academic & Professional

The Church Leader's Handbook: A Guide to Counseling Families and Individuals in Crisis

© 2009 by William R. Cutrer

Published by Kregel Publications, a division of Kregel, Inc., P.O. Box 2607, Grand Rapids, MI 49501.

The author and publisher are not engaged in providing medical or psychological services, and this book is not intended as a guide to diagnose or treat medical or psychological illness. If medical, psychological, or other expert assistance is needed, the reader is urged to seek the services of a qualified professional.

Library of Congress Cataloging-in-Publication Data
Cutrer, William.
    The church leader's handbook : a guide to counseling families and individuals in crisis / William Cutrer.
    Includes bibliographical references.
    1. Pastoral counseling. 2. Crisis intervention (Mental health services) I. Title.
BV4012.2.C88   2009   253.5—dc22   2009002842

ISBN 978-0-8254-2429-8

Printed in the United States of America

09 10 11 12 13 / 5 4 3 2 1

Crossing the Bar

Sunset and evening star,
And one clear call for me!
And may there be no moaning of the bar,
When I put out to sea,

But such a tide as moving seems asleep,
Too full for sound and foam,
When that which drew from out the boundless deep
Turns again home.

Twilight and evening bell,
And after that the dark!
And may there be no sadness of farewell,
When I embark;

For tho' from out our bourne of Time and Place
The flood may bear me far,
I hope to see my Pilot face to face
When I have crossed the bar.

—Alfred Lord Tennyson

*In memory of my father, Ben K. Cutrer,
and his father, Bennie B. Cutrer,
who both found great comfort in this poem
and now live in the presence of their "Pilot," Jesus Christ.*

*To those called of God to minister His grace to people
in the midst of a life crisis. May He bless you with a sense
of His presence, His power, and His pleasure as you
serve as a willing instrument in His hand, to His glory.*

CONTENTS

Acknowledgments

The impetus for this project began with a request from several churches for a practical manual to equip pastors, deacons, and volunteers for ministry in crisis situations. My thanks for the encouragement of Sojourn Church and Dr. Robert Cheong for getting this project off the ground.

Special thanks are due the students of the Southern Baptist Theological Seminary who have followed the call of Christ and are training to serve the Lord. In particular, several students contributed significantly in the research and writing of this project: Sara Collins, Teddi Embrey, Michael Foreman, Rob Guilliams, and Russell Webb. Class discussions and case material derive from the Biblical Counseling in Human Crises course. The lively discussions and research papers arising from this class contribute substantially to the practicality and realism of this manual.

My deep gratitude extends as well to my wife, Jane, who painstakingly proofed and edited this manuscript.

Introduction
to Crisis Care

What crises have you faced? A car accident? A disease that struck you or a loved one? Marital conflict? Infertility? Unemployment? Extreme parent-child conflict? The suicide of a loved one? Whatever difficulties you've been through, hopefully you haven't had to face them alone. The Bible tells us that two are better than one (Eccl. 4:9–12), and it's important to know we can face crises as a community of faith.

Each of us has experienced pain, is broken in some way, and lives with unfulfilled longings. Such trials are never enjoyable, yet they uniquely qualify us to "come alongside" others who hurt and provide comfort and strength. Often when we see a marriage in trouble, a person contemplating suicide, or someone struggling with a terminal illness, our first response is to think we need to call in the pastoral staff or professional counselors. But studies show that laypeople can and do help, often as capably as professionals. A caring, faithful brother or sister in Christ can be used effectively by God in crisis situations. The purpose of this manual is to give each person called to ministry some tools to be that Spirit-filled companion who provides care when someone—whether friend, family member, or church member—faces a crisis. For the purposes of this book, the term *minister* is used to denote *one doing ministry*. This may be the pastor, an assistant pastor, a seminarian, a deacon, or any spiritually mature lay leader.

As one ministers to another, crisis care is simply love in action. The Lord tells us that people will know we are Christians by our love (John 13:35). And as loving, humble servants, we help others in crisis by willingly entering into their grief and sorrow. In his letter to the Romans, the apostle Paul charges his readers to weep with those who weep (12:15), feeling their pain with them. In his letter to the Philippians, he also tells Christ-followers to consider others' needs as more important than their own (2:3). Meeting soul-care needs requires the sacrifice of our time, emotions, and sometimes even our physical resources. We are to follow the example of the footwashing Christ, identifying needs and then doing what we can to meet them.

Crises take many forms. Some happen in a moment—unexpected, inescapable, unavoidable—as with a car accident. Some happen over time—gradually, insidiously, unrelentingly—as with infirmities that come with age or a marriage that slowly deteriorates. Either way, the normal, expected flow of life is dramatically altered. Over the course of a lifetime, each of us faces crises—no-turning-back episodes that leave permanent marks.

It would be a mistake to say *the* reason God allows suffering is because it teaches us to comfort others. Yet a by-product of trials is that the One who comforts us in trouble can use us to encourage others in trouble "with the comfort with which we ourselves are comforted by God" (2 Cor. 1:4).

The Bible tells us that from the perspective of heaven each human crisis happens with God's full knowledge and permission. Each trial has some purpose. So we minister with the confidence that the Lord is in control and has His reasons. In each difficulty both the sufferer(s) and the caregiver(s) have the opportunity to be transformed into Christlikeness.

As a physician, I have experienced many moments when I've needed to communicate "the news"—words that I knew would irrevocably change everything about the hearer's life: "It's cancer," or "I suspect the coma is permanent," or "Your loved one has died." In my years as a deacon and in full-time pastoral service, I've faced similar times when I've had to speak life-changing words—whether about marriage and divorce, domestic violence, or sexual exploitation—that shattered the hearers' lives. I now have the sacred privilege of teaching the course Biblical Counseling in Human Crises at the Southern Baptist Theological Seminary in Louisville, Kentucky, and I am indebted to my students for their willingness to share their insights and research to make this handbook possible. Drawing on their experiences and mine, I hope to encourage and strengthen you in your call to minister to brothers and sisters in Christ in their dark hours of desperate need.

When it comes to caring for persons in crisis, you will find a variety of approaches: a biblical counseling model; a relational model; a medical model; and even a soul-care approach. Each of these has value in certain settings, but foundationally my purpose is to ground this work solidly on the Word of God and the practical application of the principles found therein. Thus you'll find Scripture verses, case studies, ministry approaches, and resources pertinent to each chapter.

Additionally, know that there are different categories of crisis. Developmental crises, such as growth through adolescence, puberty, and adulthood to old age, will not be the emphasis. Neither will the focus be on the so-called existential crisis of "Why am I here?" and "What was I made to do?"

Christ will never leave you or forsake you, so when you—full of God's Spirit—enter the pain of one in crisis, ministry happens through you. To the person in agony, you represent the "presence of God," which communicates in a powerful way that God cares. When a member of the body suffers, we all suffer. When we join that person in the crisis, the burden is shared and thus made lighter. As recorded in Matthew 11:29–30, Jesus said, "Take my yoke . . . my yoke is easy and my burden is light" (NIV). That is

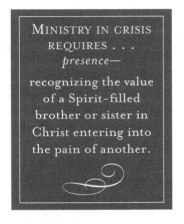

MINISTRY IN CRISIS
REQUIRES . . .
presence—
recognizing the value of a Spirit-filled brother or sister in Christ entering into the pain of another.

because Jesus *shares in the yoke*. He is taking up the burden of whatever He calls us to endure. When you, as pastor, deacon, volunteer, or friend, arrive on the scene, many will take comfort in the mere fact that you have shown up. Never underestimate the power of "presence." By "showing up" I don't mean a quick "flyby" visit, zooming in and then out of a person's world. Rather, I mean a long-term commitment— perhaps shared as a team of ministers—entering into a relationship in which you accompany another on the path to healing, to restoration, or to death's door.

I am assuming each reader has some maturity in Christ that involves a history of walking with Him and knowing His Word, that he or she prays meaningfully and regularly, and that he or she has some experience with loss. Though I may not say it at every juncture, every encounter you have with a person in crisis requires total dependence upon the Lord. Prayer is the preparation, the connection, and the sustenance that will enable you to be effectively used to God's glory. So, pray. Pray before, during, and after each ministry visit. Pray *for* the hurting, and pray *with* them, so that the person in need and you yourself may know and experience the love of God even in the midst of the suffering.

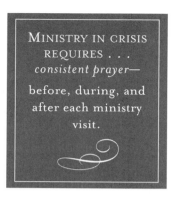

MINISTRY IN CRISIS REQUIRES . . . *consistent prayer—* before, during, and after each ministry visit.

MINISTRY IN CRISIS REQUIRES . . . *patient listening and measured words.* Even as the pain and concerns are voiced, the Spirit of God who indwells you, and perhaps the one in crisis, can minister God's grace to the broken heart.

Motivation and attitude are important. In Colossians 3:17 we read, "Whatever you do in word or deed, do it all in the name of the Lord Jesus." It is essential that your focus in ministry is not on gaining something for yourself but on honoring Christ. It's important to avoid viewing yourself as the "expert" who brings advice, solutions, and insight. Rather, come in humility, as a servant of God, a fellow pilgrim with your own frailties and weaknesses. Think beyond "sympathy," feeling sorry *for*, and even beyond "empathy," feeling sorry *with*. Rather, recognize crisis visits as divine appointments in which the Lord can lavish His grace through you upon the person in pain. In times of crisis your words will carry much less weight than the love demonstrated by your presence. Be slow to speak so that you do not injure, but, in the proper time, let the Spirit bring words of truth to the situation.

Crisis counseling has some inherent dangers. The minister's motivation can be sinful or self-serving. Some enter others' crises as opportunities to work through their own issues. While no one has reached perfection, the person in crisis must be the focus, not the ministering individual's own problems. Likewise, some seek to help out of mere curiosity about others' intimate issues. Such "counselors" want information or the control that such knowledge may bring. Others enjoy "fixing people," solving their problems, and telling others what to do. Sadly, some minister in crisis situations because they have no strong relationships of their own and doing so provides a false sense of friendship that gives them an avenue through which to soothe their own loneliness. Still others like the feeling of having people emotionally dependent upon them. You need a right heart, fully dependent upon the Lord, seeking His glory in

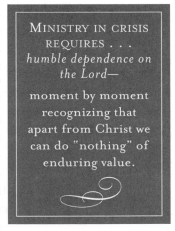

MINISTRY IN CRISIS REQUIRES . . . *humble dependence on the Lord—* moment by moment recognizing that apart from Christ we can do "nothing" of enduring value.

every word spoken and every action undertaken. We must pray for the humility never to use anyone else's suffering as a workshop; as Eugene Peterson puts it, never "cobble together makeshift, messianic work that inflates our importance and indispensability."[1]

Crisis ministry is an immensely intimate experience. Feelings will be strong as you enter into the depths of a person's pain, the rawness of a person's experience. This brings a level of transparency and trust that can be essential to the healing process but also holds potential danger for the self-confident minister. The time required between the initial visit and the reestablishing of pre-crisis relationships can take weeks, months, and even years. While the Christian love you develop will remain, the intensity should subside as life returns to normal; and it will do so, provided such feelings are not continually "fed." The person who comes to you for help in crisis should understand that your investment of love and time will focus on him or her for a season, but eventually you will need to be available to others who have needs as well. Be forewarned about the powerful emotions that can develop in you toward the person in need and vice versa.

Know that you are not alone as you minister. Not only does the Lord go with you, but you also have access to the resources of the faith community. There are probably others whom God would use in any particular situation. Engage them or refer appropriately. Create a team ministry.

---

1. *Subversive Spirituality* (Grand Rapids: Eerdmans, 1997), 167–68.

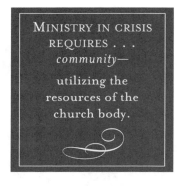

MINISTRY IN CRISIS
REQUIRES . . .
community—

utilizing the
resources of the
church body.

Surround yourself with people who have permission to ask you difficult questions about your motives. And be vigilant about establishing well-set boundaries and staying accountable to others so that you do not abuse your position of respect and authority. You represent the presence of Christ in this hurting person's life. Conduct yourself in such a way that the name of Christ is glorified.

Your participation requires humility, gentleness, and a compassion that, while it includes empathy, goes far beyond it into the spiritual realm of soul care. As Paul exhorts us in Ephesians 4:32, "Be kind to one another, compassionate, forgiving one another, just as God in Christ also forgave you." This participation comes with a cost. You may pay a high price emotionally and spiritually for choosing to get involved. Ministering—and ministering *well*—in the name of the Lord will take your full concentration and require your energy and attention. Be prepared!

PART 1

PREPARING FOR CRISIS CARE

BASIC STRATEGIES FOR CRISIS CARE

Have you ever wanted to comfort someone but didn't know what to say? How should we talk to people in crisis? How do we get to the truth, the real issues, the source(s) of the pain? How do we move from that point to healing and reconciliation? How can we honestly and compassionately prepare people and families for dying and death?

Every Christ-follower—whether a shepherd, a deacon, or servant of the Lord in a nonleadership role—is entrusted with the awesome privilege of meeting others at moments of crisis. Some believers are skilled in this arena naturally—even supernaturally. Others must work hard to establish rapport and to provide genuine empathy.

Each of us can respond with grace when God divinely appoints a meeting with another in need. One student enrolled in Biblical Counseling in Human Crises confessed that he felt no particular connection with people in crisis, believing a "good dose of Scripture" should suffice. His honesty is commendable, and his inexperience and ignorance of soul care is correctable. It's not enough to quote Scripture or proclaim it in pulpits. The gospel also must be lived out and lived into the lives of others. The love of God became embodied in Christ, not merely through stone tablets; and the Spirit of God resides in today's believer as a testimony to His grace and love.

Crisis ministry is not all that complicated. In His Upper Room Discourse (John 13), Jesus issued a new commandment that we "love one another" even as He has loved us. This is the way others will know we are Christ's disciples—by the love we have for each other. This love—the selfless, sacrificial, other-centered "agape" love—becomes the means of crisis care. The ability to love this way is a gift of God through the indwelling Holy Spirit.

Each human being's time on earth can be viewed as a journey. From the first cell to our last heartbeat, we experience joys and sorrows, triumphs and tribulations. Yet God gives us to one another to accompany, to encourage, and to bring joy and meaning to our temporal lives. When crises arise, and they will, God has given us the church, the body of Christ, to join us in carrying our burdens, helping us to make it through.

BE PRESENT

Practically, crisis care begins with human-to-human interaction. Words generally follow, but they may not always be part of this ministry—and certainly not the most important part. In fact, sometimes they can do more harm than good. Consider the parent who lost a child and heard someone say that "heaven was incomplete without her." It left him wondering why God, who can make anything, couldn't create a different child to complete heaven. Another man who was grieving the loss of his brother was told after three months, "You need to be getting over it." Rather than "wise" words, the loving presence of a fellow believer in moments of crisis remains the most important soul connection. So your interaction begins with your presence. As Ecclesiastes 4:9–12 says,

> Two people are better than one, because they can reap more benefit from their labor. For if they fall, one will help his companion up, but pity the person who falls down and has no one to help him up. Furthermore, if two lie down together, they can keep each other warm, but how can one person keep warm by himself? Although an assailant may overpower one person, two can withstand him. Moreover, a three-stranded cord is not quickly broken.

Yet what should we do once we are "present"? First, we pray. Paul exhorts his readers to pray without ceasing (1 Thess. 5:17). And for what should we pray? We should pray for the felt need, such as comfort, healing, and safety, but also for the deeper need—that the saints might be filled with "the knowledge of his will in all spiritual wisdom and understanding" (Col. 1:9). Rather than arriving as the person with every answer who will solve all mysteries, you first should approach God with an attitude of humility. James reminds us, "Humble yourselves before the Lord and he will exalt you" (James 4:10). And the prophet Isaiah wrote, "I show special favor to the humble and contrite, who respect what I have to say" (Isa. 66:2). Prayerfully wait on the Spirit of God to direct you and the conversation. Certain communication skills and styles can be helpful, but a right heart is essential.

Meaningful change and spiritual transformation come from a genuine encounter with Christ through His truth. So foundationally, we should have a good understanding of the flow of Scripture and God's desire for holiness and humility. We encourage people by expressing the love of God and our confidence that His grace can draw them to greater faith, even in the midst of trials. God is sovereign and holy. The sum total of all of His attributes constitute the weight of His glory. We serve a mighty God who is able, in all circumstances, to glorify Himself even through the severest of trials. Thus, our confidence resides in God. Our focus must be on Him, not on the circumstances that confront us. These very circumstances have brought about the crisis that provides an opportunity to glorify God.

EXPLORE THE HISTORY

Let's assume someone comes to you to talk about a marriage in crisis. As you try to understand the difficulty (if it's not readily apparent), begin discussion with some background information. Find out where and how this person grew up, discern key relationships and experiences throughout the person's lifetime, and seek to determine what factors led to the current situation. Gain an understanding of the events, not to excuse sinful behavior or choices, but to understand the background and to see if a recurring pattern has developed over a lifetime.

It's important to understand that the first problem a person in crisis mentions often is not the real problem. The real problem generally reveals itself over time. You must first develop trust before the real struggles are shared.

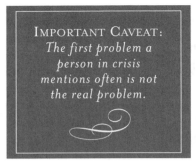

IMPORTANT CAVEAT: *The first problem a person in crisis mentions often is not the real problem.*

When I served as a senior pastor, a wife came to me seeking resolution of marital conflict, which she attributed to her husband being "too involved" at the church and neglecting his home life. Over time as the story unfolded, however, conversations revealed an overriding sense of fear on her part and ultimately the admission of ongoing domestic violence. The wife's genuine hurt was that the church had not recognized or responded to her abuse but instead had advanced and given spiritual responsibilities to a man who was yielding to sinful anger.

FOCUS ON PRESENT CONCERNS

It is generally wise to give appointments a time frame of thirty minutes or one hour so that you can focus the conversation on the need. Yet, in certain situations, such as grieving a loss or a new and profound depressive episode, time flexibility is a must.

Once you've established a level of trust, move from the historical events to the present. Ask, "What is happening now?" or "What brings you in to see me today?" Use broad, open-ended questions that can give the individual an opportunity to explore and expand on the cause. Find out how relationships are going. Ask what has changed or is changing to bring about the current situation.

The questions are to focus on the "presenting problem" as it is called in medical practice, or the "chief complaint." People have many woes, so it is important to understand what they see as the main issue. One of the first lessons in medical school is that when taking a patient's history, if you will listen carefully and not interrupt, the patient will tell you what is really wrong. When it comes to soul care, the diagnosis often can be made by hearing the "soul story." So, be patient.

How do you listen effectively? You do so by giving the person the respect and dignity that a child of God deserves. Your attention should be undivided! No phone interruptions, computer screens, shuffling papers, text messaging, looking at your watch, or scoping out the exit. For these moments, the person in front of you is your solitary focus.

Communicate by your actions that you genuinely care about the person's problem, that you are sympathetic, empathetic, and spiritually attuned to the crisis in which he or she is immersed.

Appropriate touch can be powerfully healing by communicating genuine concern. Such touch must not be threatening or have sexual overtones, and may vary somewhat in different cultural settings. Gently patting a shoulder or grasping a hand generally communicates properly. Exercise caution, however, until you have established proper rapport and understand the crisis thoroughly. If the situation involves domestic violence, touch can be very threatening; if the situation involves grieving the death of a loved one, appropriate touch may be essential to demonstrating Christian love. Anyone ministering in crisis situations must always conduct themselves in a manner consistent with godliness, that is, to remain above reproach in all situations.

Provide soft eye contact that connects rather than staring through the person. This both aids the listening process and encourages deeper sharing. Respond both verbally and nonverbally with body posture and facial expressions that invite and comfort. If you aren't sure how to do this, have a conversation with someone skilled in counseling, and ask! You may have some nervous mannerisms you don't even realize, which can shut down meaningful conversation.

Keep in mind James's admonition to be "quick to listen, slow to speak, slow to anger" (James 1:19). Sadly, for the sake of time, ministers often offer advice and counsel before they truly understand all the factors involved in a person's crisis. It takes time to draw out the person with broad, open questions, progressing smoothly to the more focused and direct ones. In many crises, this understanding takes place over several visits.

Finally, when appropriate, bring relevant Scripture to bear on the issue. Comfort when appropriate, and confront when the situation demands a truth that runs counter to the individual's thinking or decision-making process. But make sure such responses are not hasty, but rather shared in love, graciously "seasoned with salt" (Col. 4:6).

COME ALONGSIDE

The basic strategy in crisis care, after you become aware of the difficulty, involves entering into the individual's pain, decreasing his or her anxiety by coming alongside, and then striving to fully understand the problem. Then, by evaluating the individual's available resources—both internal and external, including his or her family, the church, and the community—outline a plan of ministry. When people recognize they are not alone, that someone cares and will walk with them through this pain, hope emerges and God is glorified.

The plan may include the involvement of multiple staff; home, hospital, or other direct encounters; and perhaps referral to people with special training in certain areas (e.g., medical, legal). Most large communities have hotlines for reporting specific abuses. Usually available 24/7, they may be able to provide more services than the church is equipped to do at a moment's notice. Some hotlines may support an agenda that runs contrary to biblical teaching, so don't assume that an individual's needs are being met without pastoral involvement. The goals are always 1) God's glory and 2) the person's recovery, restoration, and/or reconciliation.

ADDITIONAL RESOURCES

Boa, Kenneth. *Conformed to His Image.* Grand Rapids: Zondervan, 2001.

MacArthur, John. *Counseling: How to Counsel Biblically.* Nashville: Thomas Nelson, 2005.

Shields, Harry, and Gary Bredfeldt. *Caring for Souls.* Chicago: Moody Press, 2001.

THE HUMAN RESPONSE TO CRISIS

The human race was created by God in His own image. While theologians differ on precisely what that image involves, all agree that we are complex in our ability to think, to feel, to desire, to dream of a future. Humanity has a range of responses to external events that encompass the physical, intellectual, emotional, and spiritual spheres. To minister effectively to people in crisis, we must understand the normal range of reactions that frequently surround the human immersed in a crisis situation. Grief, depression, and anxiety are perhaps the most common coping mechanisms when facing severe stress.

GRIEF

> Now we do not want you to be uninformed, brothers and sisters, about those who are asleep, so that you will not grieve like the rest who have no hope. (1 Thess. 4:13)

Grief is a natural emotional response to loss. Though perhaps associated most commonly with death, a person can experience grief in response to many other losses. To a teenager who has experienced a "relationship failure," to a person whose beloved pet has died, or to someone fired from the "job of his dreams," grief is real and profound. For an understanding of the intensity of grief, we will focus on the death of a loved one in this section.

Scripture About Grief

We see many examples of grief in the Bible. One of the most significant figures is Job. After losing his livestock, servants, children, and health, he refused to curse God, as his wife had advised. He worshiped God in the midst of his devastation; and yet without shortchanging the emotional expression of his pain, he tore his robe, shaved his head, sat in ashes, and was so visibly distressed that his friends were speechless. Scripture testifies that "in all this Job did not sin" (Job 1:22; 2:10). In fact, from a crisis-counseling perspective, Job's friends ministered best when they spoke least. The days of silence, after these men showed up to be with Job in his pain, picture the central importance of the ministry of presence. When these friends chose to speak, being "more sure than right," they presumed on the origin of Job's suffering. That is, they attributed Job's calamity to some sin. They believed God was judging Job for secret disobedience. It is often hard to resist this conclusion when ministering to a grieving individual, but God keeps His counsels hidden most times, and the wise course is to provide the comfort and strength of a loving presence. At times words are unnecessary and may even cause additional pain.

Begin your ministry to the grieving by merely communicating how sorry you are for their loss. And even if you have experienced a similar tragedy, do not presume that you know how that person feels. You simply do not. Each of us grieves individually, in unique and specific ways. So recognize that the pain is profound, and, through prayer, carry it to the throne of grace.

Though Scripture testifies to Job's innocence in his expression of grief, not all grief is, in fact, sin-free. Sin taints all aspects of life, and grief is no exception. Not only do we grieve in a fallen world, but we also grieve as fallen creatures. Having said this, our primary concern when ministering to someone in grief is to offer compassion, comfort, and support. Correction for the grieving should be done with only the utmost caution, lest suffering be compounded.

Having taken on human form in the Incarnation, Jesus knew grief well during His time on earth. He was despised and rejected by people; He experienced pain and was acquainted with grief (Isa. 53:3). He also pronounced blessing on those who mourn (Matt. 5:4) and wept at the tomb of Lazarus, even though He knew that He would raise His friend from the dead (John 11:4, 32–36). He wept over Jerusalem (Luke 19:41) because of the sin and disobedience of God's people, and He entreated God in anguish in the garden of Gethsemane as He anticipated the cross (Matt. 26:37–44; Mark 14:33–36; Luke 22:41–44). Our Savior expressed the full range of human emotions during His sojourn here.

The examples of Christ and Job demonstrate that profound expressions of grief do not run counter to righteousness.[1] While we are not to grieve as those who have no hope (1 Thess. 4:13), an important commonality we share with the unbelieving is that *we do grieve.*

Sources of Grief

A variety of losses can lead to profound grief—death, fractured relationships, destroyed dreams, the grief of a friend, failure, loss of skills or mobility, and relational losses from relocation. The list could go on. Grief can be as recognizable as the emotion evoked upon the death of an aged parent or something as silent and invisible as the onset of menopause for a single female. Often grief accompanies those in long-term counseling as they come to terms with losses—perhaps mourning the father they never had or mourning the far-reaching consequences of choices they made. Grief can result from watching a loved one make self-destructive choices and being unable to stop him or her, or from persevering in a difficult marriage with a spouse who shows no incentive to change. The upheaval of one's parents' divorce can bring grief, as can a broken engagement. Grief can come from any great number of things that are "not the way they're supposed to be."

The Experience of Grief

Though typically thought of as an emotional experience, grief also can have physiological effects. A person may experience respiratory distress—finding breathing difficult, gasping, or expressing deep sighs. He or she may feel tightness in the throat or abdomen, feel nauseated, or notice significant changes in appetite. Additionally, the grieving person may feel weak, lacking energy or muscular strength. Many complain of pain—diffuse, difficult-to-localize aching that simply will not go away.

---

1. This is also seen in many other righteous saints, such as Paul (Acts 20:37), David (see the Psalms), and Jeremiah (see Jeremiah and Lamentations).

In the case of a lost loved one, the grieving person may occasionally imagine seeing or hearing the deceased, or dream vividly about him or her.

At an emotional level, grief is experienced as mental anguish, including shock (not the medical shock of low blood pressure but rather a surreal sense that nothing makes sense, that this cannot really be happening), numbness, sorrow, and anxiety. Such mental anguish can compromise one's ability to think rationally. A grieving person also may display selective and incomplete memory. Shock is a common component of grief, even in the event of the slow and expected death of a loved one who was terminally ill. Anxiety may stem from the stress and sorrow of separation or express the struggle against accepting our human finitude in the face of suffering. In the case of intense grief, a person may have suicidal thoughts. A loss suffered by a family will put stress on family relationships, as people tend to experience and deal with grief differently. Children may express grief by irritable moods, regression to immature behaviors, or opposition to authority. Recognize that children do grieve and do so deeply; it just manifests itself in different ways.

Abnormal Grief: Cause for Concern

There is a wide spectrum of normal grief expression, but some ways of handling grief are abnormal. Normal grief includes disrupted life rhythms, anger, guilt, and a variety of physical and emotional symptoms. These may last six months to a year following a significant loss. One should begin to see some improvement, however, as the months unfold.

Abnormal grief, which will not naturally resolve, includes symptoms such as psychosis (seeing and hearing things that are not there), complete denial of the pain, or obsession with the loss. Some people make "shrines" out of the room or belongings of the deceased. While there is no rush to remove reminders of the deceased, making such objects "sacred" can signal a dangerous grieving process.

Grief is indeed a process that is often slow and agonizing. It can be helpful to think of it in terms of common grief "stages," such as initial shock/denial, followed by anger/depression. Some bargain instead of getting angry, trying to "strike a deal" with God to make things the way they were. Ultimately a new reality emerges in that the deceased takes a new place in the memory of the grieving survivor. A new rhythm develops that some refer to as "acceptance," or "healing," which includes a return to regular activities. In her classic work based upon extensive interviews with the terminally ill as death was approaching, Kübler-Ross identified five stages in facing one's own death: (1) denial, (2) anger, (3) bargaining, (4) depression, and (5) acceptance.[2] The length and intensity of the grief process will vary from person to person and is influenced by multiple factors, including the degree to which the loss was anticipated, the magnitude of the loss, and the grieving person's personality makeup and faith system. The stages are not "mandatory," of predictable length, or logically ordered. But knowledge of this general progression can assure the counselor that progress is being made through the grief.

Ministry to the Grieving

As members of the body of Christ, we minister God's presence to each other. Pastoral care has a particular capacity to symbolize the presence of God to a grieving person. This *ministry of presence* is a central part of caring for the grieving. In a very real sense, half the job (or more!) is simply *showing up* and *being with* people in their pain.

Early contact with the grieving individual(s) communicates care for and recognition of the significance of their loss and will aid future healing. As a minister on behalf of the church, you are naturally expected to initiate contact. In the ministry of presence, connection is made through compassion, authentic empathy, and genuine respect. Ask open-ended questions and *listen*. It is important for those who are grieving to have the opportunity to verbalize their negative emotions, and a genuine listening ear can do much to encourage this expression. Repression of such emotional expression early in the process may lead to greater disturbance in the future. Be aware of all members of the family, and be careful not to overlook children. They may not understand as much of what is going on, but they are picking up on much more than their behavior may indicate. Don't be afraid to get down on their level and talk to them.

You will be ministering not only to emotional needs but to spiritual needs as well. Offer to pray with people. Sharing Scripture is

---

2.   Elisabeth Kübler-Ross, *On Death and Dying* (New York: Simon and Schuster, 1997).

also appropriate, but be careful here. Scripture can be offered prematurely in a way that shuts down emotional expression. Be sure that when you share Scripture it is genuinely for the other person's good and not a means of shielding yourself from the intense emotions of the grieving one. It is also important to be aware that although the experience of grief raises many difficult questions—which may often be verbalized to you—grieving people are not looking

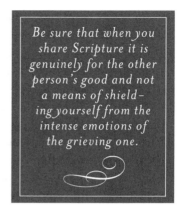

Be sure that when you share Scripture it is genuinely for the other person's good and not a means of shielding yourself from the intense emotions of the grieving one.

for instant answers. They may ask for an answer, but their heart cry is for the return of the loved one. What you can offer is empathic understanding, comfort, reassurance, personal presence, and hope, framed in a biblical view of time and eternity.

Grief is a journey, and people need company on that journey. Some have described the process as "work" needing to be done, like rehab after surgery. It is a fitting image—that of helping a brother or sister in Christ accomplish the necessary "grief work" to heal the soul. Practical strategies to suggest for processing grief include thinking reflectively, journaling, talking through the memories, weeping, and remaining involved in life-affirming relationships and the spiritual disciplines (prayer, meditation, and directed Bible study may have appropriate times). The Psalms can be especially helpful in this journey, providing people with words to voice their pain and confusion to God. Encourage them to "pour out [their] heart like water before the face of the Lord" (Lam. 2:19).

A very common question of individuals ministering to those in grief is, How long is it OK to grieve? It depends. Duration is not as important as not getting stuck. The question is not so much, Is this taking too long? but, Are we still moving ahead?

As people journey through their grief, they will grow stronger and gradually need you less. Your flexibility and ability to recognize their progress and decreased need for you is an important part of their being able to move on. At the same time, recognize that loneliness is still a major problem for most people at one year. A card or note at anniversary dates of the loss is a wonderful way to evidence continued caring as people move on.

If you have not personally experienced much grief, consider asking someone who has to talk with you about his or her experience. Let this person be your teacher. This will be an invaluable experience, not only in learning about grief, but also in increasing your comfort level in talking with individuals about such an emotion-laden topic.

Depression

> I am exhausted as I groan; all night long I drench my bed
> in tears; my tears saturate the cushion beneath me. (Ps. 6:6)

Depression affects the whole person. Many think in terms of the "ABCs of Depression"—that is, the affect (feeling), behavior (doing), and cognition (thinking). Depression impacts all areas—the physical, intellectual, emotional, and spiritual—to a significant degree.

Regarding *affect*, a depressed person's emotions evidence a deep sadness, helplessness, despair, and/or irritability. Feelings of worthlessness and hopelessness dominate. The struggle of depression can lead to an overwhelming sense of guilt and shame. Clearly, all relationships suffer. Both the spiritual life and human relationships are damaged. Spiritual disciplines such as reading the Bible and prayer often seem dry and pointless. This may lead to feelings of distrust, anger, and even hatred toward God. In such dark moments, the individual may sense only disapproval and condemnation from the Lord.

Regarding *behavior*, depression can cause a significant loss of energy and lack of desire to do anything. Depressed persons often have difficulty eating properly, sleeping, or even getting out of bed. Simple tasks such as routine hygiene may seem an overwhelming undertaking. The depressed individual may try to withdraw from human contact for extended periods. Appetites are affected. Depressed people generally consume too little or too much. Libido often disappears. In fact, most activities that the depressed person previously enjoyed doing no longer hold interest or pleasure.

Regarding *cognition*, depression often deeply disturbs thought processes. Memories are difficult to recall; focus and attention span suffer.

Decision-making ability is gone. Thoughts are often slowed, though in certain individuals the mind may race with a "pressure of ideas" and forced speech such that it may exhaust the one who tries to listen and follow the line of thinking.

Causes of Depression

As of this writing, "depression" describes a collection of symptoms, not an objective diagnosis based on a particular lab value or scan. The pain of depression can be intense, lasting from short periods to months or even years. Many theories surround depression, ranging from genetic causes, familial circumstances, neurochemical imbalances, and even sinful behavior. Volumes of research point to a many-factored cause of this symptom complex we call depression. There are neurochemical changes; serotonin, norepinephrine, and dopamine *do* play a role. Whether the changes cause the depression or result from the depression remains to be precisely determined, but considerable current medical effort seeks to discover the origins of debilitating depression so that the treatments might be more effective and specific.

Some depressions are closely tied to precipitating events. Postpartum depression, for example, can be remarkably severe, causing separation from the infant, husband, family, and friends. Many women suffer depressive symptoms after childbirth but relatively few progress to full-blown postpartum depression (symptoms lasting more than two weeks). Such patients need medical consultation as research has identified clear ties between dramatic hormonal changes and the severe symptoms, particularly in families where other members have struggled with depression. The rare cases of postpartum psychosis—with delusions, hallucinations, and suicidal and/or homicidal thoughts—remind us of the fragility of the human form.

Another type of depression with an identifiable cause is seasonal affective disorder (SAD), with symptoms generally limited to the winter months. Apparently, in some cases mood changes can be related to environmental change.

Depression certainly can be the result of sin, caused by the guilt and shame that follow poor choices. Thus the minister must listen well to fully understand what is happening within the person in crisis. Recognizing a strong family history of depression may give important clues as to who may be at greatest risk and who may need to be referred for consultation with a physician.

Current understanding of mood disorders focuses on extremes: the low, hopeless, helpless feelings of depression and the high, hyperenergetic, overproductive, creative "manic." Some "in-betweens" exist, but these two states are the two ends or "poles" of the spectrum. Thus, a "bipolar" person has both depressive and manic phases. Treatments differ for those with pure depression versus individuals suffering from bipolar disorder. There are strong family tendencies often seen in bipolar persons. Pay very close attention to the family's history of any sort of mental disorder, treatment, and/or hospitalization for this type of diagnosis.

Depression also can have a physiological connection with certain hormonal abnormalities, particularly low thyroid production. Most individuals who are stressed beyond their capacity and/or those who suffer from sleep deprivation, exhaustion, or serious life events will experience some of the symptoms of depression. Thus, the symptoms of depression are a very common part of the human experience. The spectrum of severity in depressive symptoms remains vast and will likely constitute a major part of crisis ministry.

Ministry Approaches

A depressed person needs the help that the community of faith brings: genuine care, concern, support, and at times direction to physicians or counselors. Notice the parallel approaches to the person suffering from grief.

- Be available.
- Be empathetic, not just sympathetic. Through empathy enter into the pain with the depressed person so that he or she will not feel isolated from you.
- Listen to the depressed person, and get to know his or her story. Crucial events or episodes reveal themselves only over time.
- Love and support the depressed person with appropriate encouraging words.
- Be patient. A depressed person may not see things clearly or correctly for a long time. Resolution likewise may take many months.

• Never encourage anyone to quit taking antidepressant medication. Abrupt cessation of certain medications can be life threatening. However, it may be appropriate to encourage depressed
individuals to discuss with their physicians the reasons for their
particular medicine, how long their doctors expect them to use
it, and any possible side effects or interactions it may have with
other medications.

Ministers take a variety of approaches to help depressed persons.
Each method uniquely affects aspects in a person's life that lead to
depression.

Biblical Counseling Model

"Biblical counseling" as a formal approach brings the truth of
Scripture to bear on the life circumstances, thoughts, attitudes, and
actions of the individual. The counselor has the sacred privilege of speaking the truth of God's words in a timely fashion to encourage or confront
as necessary. This approach parallels the cognitive/behavioral therapy in
the secular world but differs in that biblical counseling has the authority
of God's inerrant Word, rather than only the logic of human capabilities.
It is appropriate to view *all* depressed persons first from the perspective of
biblical revelation, as sinners saved by grace or as lost souls suffering the
effects of sin. This approach may be effective by itself or at times benefit
from the addition of physician-prescribed and -monitored medications.

Relational Models

Relational models of counseling focus on the interactions a depressed
person has with others. This approach seeks to address any sinful or
unhealthy ways a person interacts with others. Some counselors specialize in family-centered relational therapy, which tries to understand
the individual in the context of all family relationships. Others examine all the depressed individual's interpersonal relationships in order to
distinguish healthy, holy relationships from those that might be harmful or destructive. This is not contrary to biblical teaching or the "biblical counseling" method, and may hold the key to understanding the
factors causing or deepening the depression.

THE HUMAN RESPONSE TO CRISIS

Psychodynamic Model

Many secular therapists and psychiatrists use the psychodynamic model, which focuses on basic internal conflicts within a person. Most forms look for poor relationships early in life that have initiated such an internal conflict and strive to help the person resolve them. Pastoral caregivers need to be alert to the spectrum of input that depressed individuals receive from various counseling services, even those that claim to be Christian. There may well be useful information gleaned from exploring unhealthy childhood experiences and relationships, not to excuse behavior but to understand patterns so that "strongholds" may be broken. Some "biblical counseling" counselors look for basic allegiances a person has that are in conflict with the person's allegiance to God.

Physiologic Model

The physiologic model focuses on treating suspected neurochemical imbalances with various medications. Many depressed individuals respond quickly to prescribed antidepressants or normalizing hormonal levels. However, such treatment requires the evaluation of a physician trained in this area. Much current research on depressive disorders has suggested that deficits in certain brain chemicals (neurotransmitters) may be responsible or at least involved in mood disorders. While there is *currently* no specific test for levels of these hormones, functional studies of the brain (CT scans, PET scans, Spect scans, and functional MRIs) show strong evidence for a connection between depression and problems in the area of neurotransmitter efficiency. Recent research suggests a biochemical marker for depression that may well help predict those who will need and respond to antidepressant medications.[3]

As mentioned, whether these neurochemicals cause depression or result from depression remains to be fully elucidated, but many depressed individuals simply cannot think properly to process and understand biblical direction without normalizing these chemicals. Some types of depression are clearly linked to body physiology and hormonal changes

3. Robert J. Donati, Yogesh Dwivedi, Rosalinda C. Roberts et al., "Postmortem Brain Tissue of Depressed Suicides Reveals Increased Gsa Localization in Lipid Raft Domains Where It Is Less Likely to Activate Adenylyl Cyclase," *Journal of Neuroscience* 28, no. 12 (March 19, 2008): 3042–50.

(postpartum depression, perimenopausal depression, depression in pre-menstrual syndrome, hypothyroid).

There are a number of classes of medications that are designed to treat depression and/or anxiety. Physicians generally "start low and go slow," so it may take some weeks before the medication's full benefit will be noticed. A patient's failure to respond right away to any of these medications or to a change in dosage may not represent medication failure. Encourage the individual to further consult with their physician if they express concerns about their medication.

Prognosis

Most people suffering from depression can be helped. The hopeless, helpless, isolated feelings do not have to be permanent. Whether medications are necessary and/or appropriate must be determined by a trained clinician with the experience and ability both to prescribe and to follow the course of the illness over time. Scriptural encouragement *always* plays a role as we each grow into conformity with Christ.

Scriptural encouragement always plays a role as we each grow into conformity with Christ.

A person can relapse into depression, sometimes when circumstances become overwhelming again, but sometimes also without any apparent precipitating cause. Relapses may be far more difficult to treat than initial difficulties, so a person acclimating well on medications should seek good medical counsel before deciding to stop treatment.

Many competent pastoral leaders are uncomfortable counseling the person who shows signs of serious depression for fear they will miss a potentially suicidal individual. See chapter 14, which will detail the continuum of risk and encourage you to get involved, ask the right questions, and refer when appropriate.

ANXIETY AND PANIC DISORDER

> Do not be anxious about anything. Instead, in every situation, through prayer and petition with thanksgiving,

tell your requests to God. And the peace of God that surpasses all understanding will guard your hearts and minds in Christ Jesus. (Phil. 4:6–7)

In addition to grief and depression, anxiety is another common human response to crisis. Estimates suggest that forty million American adults ages eighteen and older suffer from anxiety disorders.[4] While almost anyone can experience anxiety from time to time as a result of life stress, a genuine "disorder" is diagnosed based on the severity and frequency of symptoms. Often alcohol and substance abuse are associated with true anxiety disorders, along with a predisposition to depression. In the past, anxiety disorders have constituted the most commonly diagnosed childhood psychiatric condition, so ministers should be familiar with its constellation of symptoms.

Symptoms

Persons suffering from excessive, acute anxiety may feel threatened at all times by their surroundings, may be socially isolated and disconnected, and often find no solid spiritual grounding. The disorder is commonly seen after traumatic episodes (break-ins, muggings, natural disasters) and is characterized by a sense of loss of control. Statistically, there seems to be a genetic tendency toward anxiety problems, but no particular gene has been isolated as yet. A genetic tendency, however, does not free the individual from responding biblically to this disorder.

A genetic tendency to anxiety does not free the individual from responding biblically to this disorder.

Children with anxiety disorders are noticeably "clingy" toward trusted adults and such children express a variety of physical complaints. Various aches and pains or stomach distresses that prevent school attendance are often the first clues. Sleep disorders are common, along with nightmares, which can result in fear that affects or inhibits friendships and social interactions.

---

4.   R. C. Kessler, W. T. Chiu, O. Demler, and E. E. Walters, "Prevalence, Severity and Comorbidity of Twelve-Month DSM-IV Disorders in the National Comorbidity Survey Replication," *Archives of General Psychiatry* 62, no. 6 (June 2005): 617–27.

Severe anxiety manifests itself as constant, often nonspecific fear, with the accompanying physical responses—hyperventilation, elevated heart rate with palpitations (pounding in the chest), gastric distress with nausea, and, at times, a fear of dying. This, collectively and condensed, may be called a "panic attack" and when recurrent is labeled as part of a "panic disorder."

When encountering a person who struggles with severe anxiety, it is always wise to consider a medical consultation. Elevated thyroid hormone, as well as other hormonal problems, can cause such physical symptoms and the fear that can accompany them. Failure to consider underlying medical issues—including nicotine, caffeine, and even substance abuse—may condemn the sufferer to far longer periods of distress than necessary. Most people, however, can be approached with biblical encouragement. Depressive symptoms may accompany the anxiety, so thorough questioning and careful listening as described previously will likely prove beneficial.

Anxiety that progresses to panic attacks should be appreciated as a definite life crisis. People genuinely believe that they are going to die from the episode they are experiencing. The fear can overwhelm them, and the accompanying physical symptoms are profoundly frightening. Estimates suggest that between four and eight million Americans are affected by panic attacks. Roughly 7 percent of our general population has experienced an isolated or occasional episode that fits the criteria of panic attack. Unfortunately, many of these people are misdiagnosed or dismissed as having an "overemotional" response to a stress or event. Untreated, these people can develop phobias that cause considerable distress.

Common symptoms of a panic attack center on an intense fright. The heart rate elevates with feelings of "pounding." Coupled with shortness of breath and dizziness, such symptoms can make the episode look like a heart attack. In fact, that's what most people initially believe is happening, and they are often taken to the emergency room believing that death is imminent. The adrenaline pumped into the bloodstream in response to the fear causes all these symptoms, along with elevated blood pressure and abdominal pain or distress. Hyperventilation can lead to numbness and tingling in the extremities that add to the sense of doom. The sufferer's thoughts race, making it very difficult to concentrate as he or she feels totally trapped and out of control.

Panic disorder often begins in early adulthood and is more commonly seen in women than men. The episodes are generally short and resolve before any treatment is actually begun, but the ten or fifteen minutes they ordinarily last seem like an eternity to the one who fears for their life.

Some medical conditions mimic this disorder, for example, a tumor that secretes adrenaline, or, as already mentioned, an elevated thyroid hormone level. If you have ever been in a "close call" car accident, your body released a surge of adrenaline, and you have had many or all of the symptoms outlined above. The "fight-or-flight" response when a wave of fear hits is very similar to what those suffering from panic attacks experience on a regular basis.

Ministry Approaches

Ministry approaches to panic attacks and anxiety disorder include, first, an understanding of how frightening these episodes are. Truly, a Christian does not live in fear but in faith, but a measure of understanding will begin the process of connecting with the person in crisis. After ruling out genuine medical emergencies, effective therapies include right thinking and right speaking. For example, Philippians 4:6 directs the believer to "not be anxious about anything," and 1 Peter 5:7 says to cast "all your cares on him because he cares for you." These can be foundational in beginning the process of right thinking about whatever the trigger might prove to be.

Once medical causes are eliminated, breathing techniques and relaxation exercises while meditating upon Scripture can be beneficial in avoiding or quickly ending the attacks. Acutely, while the person is in such distress and afraid another attack is "around the corner," some medications have been effectively prescribed to get ahead of the disorder. Particularly if the person has suffered for many months or years with panic attacks, occasionally getting some measure of success by stabilizing the neurochemical environment may be appropriate.

Certain lifestyle measures have been beneficial, including proper diet, exercise, and rest. God has designed us to need rest and nourishment in appropriate measure. Restful sleep can be one of God's greatest graces. Avoidance of stimulants (caffeine, nicotine, alcohol, and nonprescribed medications) can make an enormous difference. Developing spiritual friendships, which may include you as a minister, likewise form the support that aids recovery.

ADDITIONAL RESOURCES
Grief
Dunn, Bill, and Kathy Leonard. *Through a Season of Grief.* Nashville: Thomas Nelson, 2004.

Holland, John, et al. *Lost for Words: Loss and Bereavement Awareness Training.* London: Jessica Kingsley Publishers, 2005.

Kaiser, Walter C., Jr. *Grief and Pain in the Plan of God.* Fearn, Scotland: Christian Focus Publications, 2004.

Lewis, C. S. *A Grief Observed.* Norwalk, CT: Easton Press, 2002.

Tada, Joni Eareckson, and Steven Estes. *When God Weeps: Why Our Suffering Matters to the Almighty.* Grand Rapids: Zondervan, 2002.

Depression
Biebel, David B., and Harold G. Koenig. *New Light on Depression.* Grand Rapids: Zondervan, 2004.

Cloud, Henry, and John Townsend. *What to Do When You Don't Know What to Do: Discouragement and Depression.* Nashville: Thomas Nelson, 2005.

Welch, Edward T. *Depression.* Winston-Salem, NC: Punch Press, 2005.

Anxiety/Panic
Hart, Archibald. *The Anxiety Cure.* Nashville: W. Publishing Group, 1999.

Stanley, Charles F. *Finding Peace: God's Promise of a Life Free from Regret, Anxiety, and Fear.* Nashville: Thomas Nelson, 2007.

VISITATION ETIQUETTE

The most common crisis ministry takes place in hospitals, funeral homes, and various extended care facilities, even homes. The very regularity of these crises offers the pastor opportunities to model crisis ministry for others—younger believers, assistant pastors, or lay leaders. The fact that this type of ministry takes place off-site provides a built-in opportunity for preparation. Use this travel time to pray and prepare for the situation as much as possible. Intentionally share your experience with a younger believer through conversational interaction as you anticipate the coming interaction. These visits represent powerful opportunities to impart and model grace. You will strengthen one another and bless those you share with in these circumstances.

HOSPITAL VISITATION

Those who seek to minister to people in crisis must be comfortable and competent in high-stress environments. Hospitals, and in particular emergency rooms, intensive care units, and other high-risk areas can be disorienting and even frightening. The minister must develop a comfort level in the midst of seeming chaos in order to be a calming, godly presence in the midst of the storms of life. In preparation for these inevitable ministry opportunities, pastors, deacons, and lay leaders should familiarize themselves with the "routine" of hospital life before being called upon in a crisis. This can best be accomplished if another more experienced pastor, the hospital chaplain, or perhaps even a doctor from the congregation can guide you through the various units to acclimate you to the various sights, sounds, and smells.

Once at ease with the presence of cardiac monitors, IV bags and tubing, catheters, and the like, you will not be distracted from the task of providing comfort and a godly presence to the patient and the family. It is not necessary to be able to read or interpret the monitor tracings, but you do not want to be agitated by the beeping or the various sounds made by ventilators and medication pumps. You will then be able to maneuver around the equipment without disturbing cords or moving the patient inappropriately. Do not sit on the bedside unless invited. There is no advantage for you to ask what each of the IV bags contains or precisely what the monitors are showing, unless you are medically trained. Certainly if the patient discusses those things or describes the treatment plan, you should listen attentively. But keep your focus on spiritual and emotional needs, and pray for wisdom for those entrusted with caring for medical needs.

Of course, if you have symptoms of cold, flu, or any potentially contagious illness, send someone else to visit! The patient's resistance is likely compromised, and you would not want to further endanger his or her health.

Pastors and spiritual representatives of the patient's church are usually given the privilege of entry during nonscheduled hours; don't abuse the privilege! *Do* knock before entering any room. Sometimes procedures are taking place that you don't want to interrupt. In the ER or ICU, quietly enter the room, quickly assess whether the patient is awake, in distress, or occupied with a test or procedure. In a ward, if the patient is sleeping or has been taken to another department for X-rays or other tests, leave a note so the patient will know of your visit. In fact, calling ahead before visiting hospitalized patients is never a bad idea. Some days they may not appreciate the visit because of the testing or preparations performed. Being hospitalized upsets the patient's world, and the minister's task is to encourage the patient, not make himself or herself feel important.

If the time seems appropriate, quietly move into the patient's view and softly greet the patient. If he or she extends a hand, certainly give it a gentle, two-handed hold. Having prayed before entering the room, let the conversation develop normally, at the patient's directive. A general question about how things are going or how the patient is feeling is appropriate. Then wait to see how the patient responds. If there is a chair, be seated. Many studies suggest that sitting conveys a sense of unhurried calm. Patients reflect that the visits always seemed longer and better when the minister relaxed, sat, and engaged in conversation. Ten or fifteen minutes is usually enough for nonfamily members, so stand up to excuse yourself, affirming to the patient that he or she needs to rest, and offer to pray. If the patient invites you to stay longer, then you are free to stay longer, but ordinarily, unless you are a close family friend, short, frequent visits fit best. Do ask if there is anything that you or the church can do for the patient while he or she is hospitalized. Often simple daily tasks are of great concern to the patient, even in the face of major illness so anticipate these and offer to arrange for them to be done.

Prayers should be brief but should include a request for the patient's strength in body, mind, and spirit. It is usually appropriate to pray for the patient's smooth and uneventful recovery in the Lord's will, though at times, a prayer of deep trust in the Lord in the situation may resonate more with the prognosis. Pray for the family, and for the medical personnel that they would be wise, discerning, kind, and compassionate. Pray that God would be glorified through this situation and that He might minister His grace to this individual.

With a warm smile and light touch (handshake, touch of arm or shoulder), you can excuse yourself from the bedside. Only rarely does the patient have a disease that is so contagious that you need to scrub, gown, and glove to enter or leave the area. Otherwise, take a hand or offer a gentle touch to appropriately communicate your love and concern. Your willingness to draw near, to reach out, to sit with the ailing one ministers love and grace in ways that words may not.

Visiting with the family in the waiting room doesn't have the same time constraints. You should stay as long as is practical for your schedule. When someone is having surgery, joining the family in the waiting room demonstrates the love of Christ beautifully. However, if the waiting room is full of friends of the family and you are not as familiar with the patient, do not feel obligated to sit through a four- or six-hour surgery as a matter of duty. Follow along with the conversation as it develops, and learn to be comfortable with silence. You are not there to entertain. Sometimes silently reflecting upon the events of the day can be strengthening to the soul. If appropriate in the family setting, offer to pray.

Learn to be comfortable with silence.

EXTENDED CARE FACILITY VISITATION

Visiting church members and their family members in extended care facilities provides a wonderful ministry opportunity as well. Simply moving to such a facility may be traumatic. Leaving behind a house with its many memories, adjusting to the new routine, and particularly the perceived lack of control can make this a very real crisis.

The circumstances and type of home will impact the approach of the minister. Some homes are assisted-living facilities with a variety of services. Nursing homes provide round-the-clock supervision and on-site medical personnel. Other facilities are staffed with "caregivers" who are not credentialed medically.

Depending on the diagnoses that brought the person to the home, the visits can range from sitting with someone with Alzheimer's or other type of dementia to a lively discussion with an individual whose mental faculties are fully intact but whose physical limitations require the assisted care. In any event, following prayerful preparation, the essence of crisis care in this setting is your presence, your patience, and your ability to engage in a conversation in keeping with the abilities of the one you are visiting. Generally, there is no time pressure, as these individuals often enjoy extended visits. Occasionally there are planned activities or procedures that might interrupt your time together.

These visits can be rotated among church staff and trained members, making the person in the extended care facility understand his or her value to the church community. These visits are relaxed, casual, and represent a genuine offering of time to God and the person you visit.

Listen well, and observe confidentiality.

While one should not directly pry into medical details, often the person you visit will outline in considerable detail all of the symptoms and events that are transpiring. Listen well, and observe confidentiality. While it is appropriate to pray with the individual, and ask permission to allow the church to pray for the person as well, medical details are best left general to avoid error and embarrassment.

Hospice care is essentially comfort care when death is deemed imminent and no further medical procedures are possible or warranted. Hospice can be involved with a patient in a hospital, a nursing home, or even at the patient's home. Whatever the setting, recognize the significance of hospice care. The goal of this type of care is a dignified, compassionate approach to keeping a patient comfortable and pain-free in the final days of life. Once a person is placed on hospice, no major medical interventions will be instituted. (More attention will be given to end-of-life decision making in chapter 15, including end-of-life directives like living wills, durable power of attorney for health care, and do-not-resuscitate orders.) Remember, even if anticipated, even if death means the end of earthly suffering, for the survivor the grief is real and often profound.

As a person approaches death, breathing patterns change, even the medications that relieve pain can cause respiratory complications. The sounds of inhaling and exhaling can be quite disturbing to the unprepared minister. The death of a believer, however, is a miraculous thing. Leaving this earthly frame to awaken in the presence of the Lord should give pause for reflection and self-examination even in the midst of this loss.

FUNERAL HOME VISITATION

All who are called to ministry will likewise need skills regarding death and funeral planning and procedures. Like the hospital setting, one must acclimate to the funeral home environment. Fortunately, the best funeral homes have well-trained directors who are very helpful in guiding the minister through the process. Meet the directors in your community. Visit the funeral homes so that you are comfortable with the layout before you are called to pray or preside at a funeral. Know the customs of the community where you serve. For some, the pastor arrives before the first visitation and stands at the head of the casket to greet the family and other mourners as they arrive. In other settings, the graveside service is not complete until the pastor removes his flower boutonniere and places it on the casket.

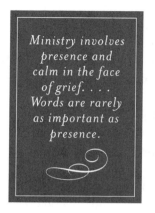

Ministry involves presence and calm in the face of grief. . . . Words are rarely as important as presence.

Generally, upon notification of death, the pastor or other staff minister goes to the hospital or home to be with the family. This should be accomplished as soon as reasonable. During this visit, ministry involves presence and calm in the face of grief. Deacons and trained leaders can provide enormous assistance to the staff and comfort to the grieving family. Words are rarely as important as presence. Good listening and reflection upon the life of the deceased usually are sufficient. Generally, a funeral-planning visit to the home of the next of kin is scheduled for the next day. This is the time to talk through, and listen well to, the stories about the deceased that will personalize the funeral message. Again, your presence is key. If you knew the deceased well, you can even contribute to the conversation. The hard times, the high times, the laughter, and the tears make this a precious ground of ministry.

Occasionally, so the family can return home to rest, one of the ministers may offer to stay with the deceased (in the hospital or nursing home) until those from the funeral home come to transport the body. This is not a waste of time but rather an offering of time to the Lord. The family will be comforted that their loved one is not "alone," and you will have freed them to rest and prepare for the profound grief that awaits them in the coming days.

Visitation at the funeral home can last for several hours. The pastor need not be present for all of it, but at the initial viewing your presence may comfort and strengthen the family as they encounter their loved one for the first time in this way. You may excuse yourself after an appropriate period of time and perhaps other members of the ministry team can take responsibility from here. If you are presiding at the funeral itself, communicate with the funeral director to clarify the times and locations for the various ceremonies.

PERIODIC HOME VISITS

All churches have an aging population because we are all aging! Prepare to continue the fellowship of the body by involving shut-ins, the disabled, and the elderly who are no longer able to travel. This represents an ongoing ministry, and while not an acute crisis like some, the need to respond and anticipate crises becomes apparent. In-home visits can be delightful, encouraging both the visitor and the one visited. And home visits provide another opportunity to model ministry for a younger believer or to involve your spouse.

Be wise as you prepare for these visits. Don't go into a situation that might compromise integrity or give the appearance of evil, but neither be afraid to minister in a legitimate crisis. Pray before you go. As a general guideline, visit in pairs and call ahead so your visit is expected. On certain occasions pastoral leaders are called to visit shut-ins alone. Should this situation arise, call ahead and notify your church office where you will be, how long you will be there, and how to contact you.

Once you arrive, quickly assess the situation for safety issues, abandonment issues, or other obvious health issues that the church might be able to address. Generally, around thirty minutes makes a good visit, shorter if the person seems fatigued or distressed by the visit. Enjoy fellowship and conversation with this individual. Ask questions about spiritual, physical, and emotional health. It may be appropriate to bring sermon material from the church, and a means to play it if necessary. Listening to the worship service via CD or iPod can bring a sense of connection with the church family.

At your initial visit to each shut-in, get the appropriate contact information should the need arise. Any family, close friend, or designated person whom you would be able to contact in an emergency. In many states, when a person is taken to a hospital, church information is obtained and the office notified. Thus, the information you have might well connect the medical staff with additional resources that would benefit the patient.

You will come to more deeply understand and appreciate others in your community (whether church members or other church related contacts) by getting into their homes.

PART 2

Ministering in
Specific Crisis
Situations

CRISIS PREGNANCY AND ABORTION

One critical conflict of our age pits the sanctity of human life against the so-called quality of human life. Sanctity implies an inestimable value and immeasurable dignity to every human being regardless of age (embryo to elderly), size (one cell to the thirty trillion cells of an average adult), mental capacity, or physical ability. Human beings are made in the image of God (Gen. 1:26–27) and as such have particular value. God Himself has declared human life sacred and commanded that such life is not to be taken.

Many argue from the perspective of "quality of life," declaring that some human lives are of greater or lesser value. This judgment arises from human reasoning toward certain individuals or certain classes of persons (e.g., embryos, the mentally or physically disabled, the elderly) and not by God's clear declaration. Thus, it is reasoned, an unwanted life, if not a "quality" life, can be terminated. For those who believe this, abortion and euthanasia make ethical and moral sense.

Writing as a pro-life physician and pastor, I strongly hold to the sanctity of human life and counsel in these types of crises from this perspective. While certain legal offenses may forfeit one's right to life (premeditated murder), life is a gift, a stewardship from God to be cherished and perhaps at times even endured for God's glory. As we explore the decisions at both the beginning and the end of life, we must do so from the perspective that life is precious. Though death is inevitable for every person until the Lord returns, each life has value and purpose.

God's Word contains numerous references to the value of each human life as made in the image of God. Because every person embodies the divine image, human beings are valued for their being, not for their function. Hence, every baby is worthy of honor, regardless of the circumstances surrounding conception. The Bible clearly teaches that having children is a desirable goal within marriage and that full sexual expression belongs exclusively within the marriage relationship. Once a pregnancy has begun, however, the choice to have premarital or extramarital sex becomes secondary to the value of the child, even though such sexual behavior is sinful and should be confronted with the goal of repentance and confession.

Additionally, every baby is worthy of dignity, regardless of possible birth defects (e.g., physical structural abnormalities or mental deficits secondary to developmental issues or infection). Even in cases of rape or incest, the infant is innocent (the mother likewise is innocent and the victim of a crime) and of immeasurable value as one who images God. Every human develops as a result of God's awesome and intimate handiwork. No pregnancy is a surprise to God (Ps. 139:13; Job 10:8–12). God has a plan for each human life, regardless of any physical and mental limitations. Scripture also affirms human personhood from the moment of conception as clearly seen in the incarnation of Jesus Christ (Matt. 1:18–24; Luke 1:26–56). "I will give you thanks because your deeds are awesome and amazing. You knew me thoroughly" (Ps. 139:14).

Scripture affirms human personhood from the moment of conception.

While not specifically mentioning "abortion," Scripture strongly and clearly condemns the taking of an innocent life. To those who lived in Old Testament times, abortion was not a consideration for God's people because the baby, while developing, was considered a "neighbor." And the people of God were commanded to love God and to love their "neighbor" as themselves. Consider Exodus 21:22–25, which grants status to the unborn. Depending on how one interprets the passage, it suggests either that a baby has status, though lesser than the mother, or that it has equal status such that if harmed by premature delivery, there is an equivalent penalty. If the infant dies, a life for a life would be required. Scripture condemns the shedding of innocent blood (Deut. 19:10; Prov. 6:17), inside and outside the womb. Scripture condemns mass killings of young children as seen in the histories of Pharaoh (Exod. 1:15–22) and Herod (Matt. 2:16). The instances in which God calls for the destruction of a nation or race, including women and children, must then be seen in light of His right to judge His people for their sinfulness.

CRISIS PREGNANCY

Since the United States Supreme Court legalized abortion through the case *Roe v. Wade* in 1973, over 40 million babies have been aborted in America. In 2005 1.21 million abortions were performed.[1] Of all abortions, 64.4 percent are performed on never married women; married women account for 18.4 percent of all abortions; and divorced women, 9.4 percent.[2] Clearly, crisis pregnancies are not uncommon and affect entire families.

Parents of young people who have conceived prior to marriage struggle with the consequences of those pregnancies. Some parents influence their daughter or son to abort the baby, in some cases even paying for it. Both the mothers and the fathers of the babies involved in such pregnancies may later grapple with the consequences of their sin. For many young people, options such as parenting the child or making an adoption plan for the child are viewed as unacceptable.

Crisis pregnancies can result from premarital or extramarital sexual exposure, rape, and incest. Within marriage, failure of a contraceptive technique may result in a "crisis" pregnancy. (A baby is never a failure but may result from failure of a contraceptive method.) Thus, some unwanted pregnancies are the direct result of sinful choices; others are not. As the medical director of A Woman's Choice, a Pregnancy Resource Center in Louisville, I regularly see women representing the entire spectrum of experiences. Many are single, but not all. Each pregnancy poses problems for the expectant mother, yet each developing

---

1. Guttmacher Institute, www.guttmacher.org (accessed November 2008).
2. The Center for Bioethical Reform, www.abortionno.org (accessed November 2008).

human has tremendous value. How should we approach these situations? How do we minister grace in the face of an unwanted pregnancy? Whom do we call for assistance?

Issues in Crisis Pregnancy

For the person involved in a crisis pregnancy, the world seems to come to a halt as she (and he) contemplates this sudden life change. Most feel afraid and alone. Some women deny they are pregnant. Some deny the baby is a person and see the pregnancy as mere fetal tissue needing extraction. Most women don't "want" an abortion, or to "kill the baby," they just don't *want* to be pregnant. The stress of the situation may render a person less likely to make an informed and caring decision.

Some common reasons given for desiring an abortion include the following:

- lack of money to raise the child
- disruption of life plans
- dissolution or deterioration of relationship with the father of the baby
- desire to avoid raising a child alone
- trauma caused by bringing into marriage a baby who is the "other man's" child
- fear of the consequences of being "discovered" as pregnant
- pain of disappointing family by having a child out of wedlock

Understanding these key issues can assist the minister in addressing the specific (and real) problem(s) that inclines a particular woman toward abortion. Remarkably, a pervasive resistance to making an adoption plan exists and must be overcome. Mothers with reservations about adoption often state that they could never "give away" their baby through adoption. They view this as abandoning their child and consider the destruction of the baby a better alternative. Often such women do not appreciate the reality and permanence of the decision to abort. They just want the crisis to be over, to not be "pregnant" any longer. Yet once the abortion is done, the decision is irrevocable (though not unforgivable). Opportunities to minister grace arise both before a decision about abortion, possibly saving a life, and after an abortion, restoring the mother through God's forgiveness and helping her to heal.

Brief Medical Considerations of Abortion

Abortion is the second most common surgical procedure performed in America. (Circumcision is number one.) Although abortions in the United States have become safer since being legalized in 1973, complications such as hemorrhage, infection, perforation of the uterus, and death still occur on occasion. Infections may result, which can lead to problems with future fertility if left untreated.

The risk of miscarriage in future pregnancies increases with two or more abortions. When an abortion is performed after the first three months of pregnancy, the risk of complications increases. Abortion methods vary. Some choose the pharmaceutical option ("emergency contraception," which includes the "morning-after pill" approach or Plan B; and RU486, which is used later when the pregnancy has been established). Others opt for surgical procedures to extract the baby from the womb (suction curettage, dilation and curettage, and dilation and evacuation). The so-called "partial birth abortion" results when the infant is delivered almost completely and then violently removed (dilation and extraction—D&X). In most states a physician's prescription is required for the pharmaceutical abortion medications mentioned, though nonprescription Plan B has become available in some locations. The surgical procedures carry potentially harmful physical risks to the woman's body and long-term emotional consequences as well.

Ministry to Those Struggling with Crisis Pregnancy

Many women in a crisis pregnancy do not want others to know. If the mother and/or father of the baby are teenagers, they are likely to conceal the pregnancy from their parents and other authority figures. So regardless of how you come to know about the crisis pregnancy, you must immediately recognize that the expectant mother/father/grandparents may not want others involved. So approaching this situation with compassion and respect are paramount in assuring them of your care for them as persons, your desire for them to have all of the facts about their options, and your desire for them to reach out to the Lord for guidance and strength.

You can provide information or refer them to a local pro-life crisis pregnancy center, where they can obtain information about physical care for themselves and the baby. Remember your responsibility to minister care for both mother *and* infant. Information about the negative physical, emotional, and spiritual consequences of abortion can be truthfully and compassionately shared. It is important for the mother of the baby to have an ultrasound to check for viability since the miscarriage rate is high and a small number of pregnancies implant in the fallopian tube (ectopic pregnancies) and represent a genuine risk to the mother's life. If the mother of the baby is abortion-minded, offer assistance in contacting either her family doctor or a local crisis pregnancy center to schedule her for evaluation and possible ultrasound. The ultrasound image and heartbeat of the baby can demonstrate the presence of a new life, not just "fetal tissue" or "products of conception."

If the mother of the baby is abortion-vulnerable (she is being pressured by her parents or the father of the baby to have an abortion), you will need to extend your ministry to the entire family. In all such cases, share the truth about the physical, emotional, and spiritual consequences of abortion to all involved in the decision-making process. An abortion will provide an immediate "solution," but it brings with it some lifelong problems. *Ninety percent* of women who have had abortions ultimately regret their decisions and wish they'd had more information with which to make an informed decision to either parent the baby or make an adoption plan.[3] Scripture repeatedly affirms the life-giving option of adoption as seen in the life of Moses (Exod. 2:1–10). Everyone who trusts Christ for salvation is adopted into the family of God; so clearly adoption is a God-honoring way of family building.

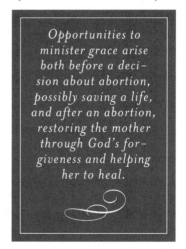

Opportunities to minister grace arise both before a decision about abortion, possibly saving a life, and after an abortion, restoring the mother through God's forgiveness and helping her to heal.

Even if the mother of the baby elects the adoption option, she will still need obstetrical care throughout the pregnancy. She also may need

---

3. Care Net, www.care-net.org (accessed November 2008).

housing, food, transportation, and other necessities if her parents reject her. The church community can step in and make a life-saving difference. Other agencies and clinics can offer support locally as well. Maternity homes and adoption agencies offer various types of assistance. If the mother of the baby decides to parent the child, both obstetrical care and pediatric care will be important. Some postbirth care is expertly provided at Necole's Place (www.awomanschoice.org) in Louisville, Kentucky, a model of ministry to those in the midst of this crisis. Each church should become familiar with the resources available to them locally.

In all such situations a personal commitment to pray for those involved in a crisis pregnancy is essential. All involved need to know someone cares about them, their baby, and their future. They need to see a future beyond the immediate crisis. Your ministry of presence and involvement lets them know they are not alone and that someone genuinely loves them regardless of the factors (e.g., sin of premarital sex, sin of sex outside of their marriage) that resulted in the crisis pregnancy. Again, they must be reminded that the baby is a separate person from the mother.

> *All involved need to know someone cares about them, their baby, and their future. They need to see a future beyond the immediate crisis.*

If the baby was conceived through the act of rape or incest, grieve with the woman over the violence done to her body, soul, and mind. She is an innocent victim of a heinous crime, and she needs comfort and reaffirmation of her value in the eyes of the Lord. An abortion violates the woman a second time. Share with her how the baby is also innocent and should be protected. The father of the baby is the guilty party, not the baby. Carrying the baby throughout the pregnancy will be difficult; however, the Lord will grant the woman grace, the church can provide support, and her faithfulness will be a testimony. Whether she chooses to raise the child herself or develop an adoption plan, this precious child has an opportunity to live.

Remind each mother of God's love and concern for her, especially during a crisis pregnancy. If the crisis pregnancy is a result of sinful sexual activity, direct the woman to 1 John 1:9, which says, "If we confess our sins, he is faithful and righteous, forgiving us our sins and cleansing us from all unrighteousness." Christianity centers on the gospel, the "good news" of Jesus Christ taking sin upon Himself and dying to provide forgiveness of sins for those who place their faith in Him. Also, as you minister in this situation, you receive the blessing of serving those in need: "Carry one another's burdens, and in this way you will fulfill the law of Christ" (Gal. 6:2).

POSTABORTION

If the statistics numbering the abortions in America include more than one million abortions per year since 1973, obviously many, many women's and men's lives have been affected by the decision to abort. Recalling the common reasons listed for abortion earlier, self-interest dominates. The pride of rebellion against God's authority over human life is the heart of sin. Money issues, lifestyle issues, interrupted plans, uncommitted relationships, fear of exposure—these are merely the rationalizations of self-centeredness. The stories that I am personally aware of regarding deacon fathers and pastors who actually encouraged or participated in the arranging of abortions are heartbreaking. We need an awareness of the breadth of this problem and a spiritual sensitivity to the wounded souls whose lives have been scarred by a decision to terminate the life of a developing child. Opportunities remain to demonstrate the love of God for our broken sisters and brothers.

The Consequences of Abortion

Scripture tells us that "all have sinned and fall short of the glory of God" (Rom. 3:23). God does not place a rank or scale upon sin with regard to salvation; however, He does allow different sins to produce consequences in this lifetime. Those who have terminated their pregnancies—the postabortive—frequently suffer guilt, shame, and grief. Having an abortion is almost without exception sin in the eyes of the Lord, for it is taking an innocent life. (In those exceedingly rare instances where the physical life of the mother is at stake, the ethical/moral question becomes less clear.)

Postabortion Syndrome (PAS) is the term used to describe the common aftereffects of abortion, including anxiety, guilt, depression (sleep disorders; helpless or hopeless feelings), spiritual deadness, flashbacks (especially on the baby's scheduled birth date or on the anniversary date of the abortion), substance abuse, and eating disorders. Estimates suggest that 65 percent of postabortive women experience profound negative effects in the years following their abortion. Early evidence concludes that postabortive women may offer lower emotional support to any future children because of their guilt over aborting a previous child. Postabortive women may have an increased risk of premature birth and miscarriage as well.[4]

The women at greatest risk for PAS are those who have been coerced into having an abortion (e.g., the father of the baby insisted on the abortion or threatened to end the relationship if the baby was not aborted; parents of the young mother insisted on the abortion or threatened eviction and loss of emotional support/love if the baby was not aborted). Young women (ages 15–24) are especially at risk for PAS. Those who are raised within a religious context are at elevated risk for PAS (the young women or their parents placed "respect of the church community" above respect for the life of the baby). Those who have had multiple abortions also are at greater risk for PAS (they often have a low view of their own value, having placed so little value on the baby). Victims of rape or incest and those who aborted an abnormal fetus are likewise at risk for PAS. Those who have had an abortion and then find themselves with infertility problems later in life are also at particular risk for PAS (for they see that their "one chance" of having a baby earlier in life was their only chance).

Ministry to the Postabortive

You can provide prayer support and factual information, and/or refer those who are suffering with PAS to a local crisis pregnancy center where they can learn about PAS. The following steps can begin the healing process:

- Help them face the truth about the abortion and *accept the loss* of the baby.

---

4.   See www.care-net.org.

- Help them address the abortion decision—*confess the sin* (e.g., circumstances, worldview).
- Help them deal with the guilt and shame and *seek forgiveness.*
- Help them *grieve the loss.* Part of the healing process is to discuss the abortion and postabortive feelings with another person and to still hear "God forgives."

Involvement with a postabortion Bible study for women may also be helpful. (Similar studies for the fathers are offered in some locales.) Many crisis centers and a few churches with support groups offer memorial services for babies lost to abortion. This has proven to be an important step for many women trying to recover from their abortion experience.

In all of these situations a personal commitment to pray for those who are postabortive is foundational. They need to know that someone cares about them, their aborted baby, and their future. They need to see a future filled with hope amid the consequences of abortion. They need to see that God has a plan for their lives, even though they have sinned against God. Remind them of God's love for them and how the Lord may present opportunities to minister to others. As the apostle Paul wrote, "Blessed is the God and Father of our Lord Jesus Christ, the Father of mercies and God of all comfort, who comforts us in all our troubles so that we may be able to comfort those experiencing any trouble with the comfort with which we ourselves are comforted by God" (2 Cor. 1:3–4).

ADDITIONAL RESOURCES

A Woman's Choice Resource Center at www.awomanschoice.org.
Care Net at www.care-net.org.
Cutrer, William R. *Choices: A Pregnancy Guide.* Morrisville, NC: Lulu Publishing, 2005.
Cutrer, William R., and Sandra Glahn. *The Contraception Guidebook.* Grand Rapids: Zondervan, 2005.
Focus on the Family at www.focusonthefamily.com.
Pierson, Anne. *Looking at Adoption: Choosing What Is Right for My Baby and Me.* www.lovingandcaring.org.

INFERTILITY

Infertility is a far more common crisis than most in ministry appreciate. More than one in six couples of childbearing age suffer from infertility. Depending on how much reproductive technology a given couple is willing and/or able to implement, perhaps as many as half of these couples will go on to experience a live birth. The emotional and financial cost, however, can be overwhelming. The strain on marital intimacy can be substantial as well. The sense of grief and loss (loss of dreams, of a jointly conceived child, of the process of pregnancy, labor and delivery, nursing, parenting the next generation) impacts every facet of their lives. Couples experiencing this crisis are faced with a whole host of issues—spiritual, marital, ethical, emotional, and medical.

Scripture contains various references to infertility, mostly by way of biblical characters who experienced it. These narratives present us with the general principle that God "opens and closes the womb," but they are not intended to be exhaustive medical texts on infertility. In fact, most of the examples of Scripture are situations in which a trial ultimately glorifies God when He breaks into an "impossible" situation (from the human standpoint) to bring about His redemptive plan. Some suggest that infertility always represents God's curse on an individual. A close examination of Scripture, however, suggests that most of the examples of infertility in the Bible were experienced by righteous women (Sarah, Hannah, Elizabeth) and fit into God's magnificent plan of doing the miraculous when, from an earthly perspective, all was hopeless. If you examine the blessings and curses in Deuteronomy, you will note that when God brings the *judgment* of infertility, all the females of the nation are barren, including the livestock![1]

What Scripture does provide is validation of the intense emotional pain of infertility. Proverbs 30:15–16 lists the barren womb among four things that are "never satisfied," that never say "enough." The story of Hannah (1 Sam. 1) gives us the closest look into the inner turmoil caused by infertility. Hannah's pain is described as bitterness of soul expressed to God in weeping prayers of anguish. She cries and feels depressed. She does not want to eat. Her husband does not understand her pain. And she cries out to God to remember her in her affliction. All such actions comprise a normal response of grief, and there is no sense from the passage that God thinks Hannah is overreacting. The desire for children is good and God-given, and when it is unfulfilled, it can cause profound pain.

On initial reading, one might think that the only cases of infertility the Bible records are in reference to women. Several passages imply male infertility, however. Ruth was childless in her first marriage but conceived soon after marrying Boaz. The levirate marriage laws make provisions for a childless woman who becomes widowed. In such cases her husband's brother is to take her as his wife and raise offspring to ensure his brother's name is carried on (Deut. 25:5–10). Scripture assumes the possibility of both male and female infertility, which is consistent with the findings of medical science.

THE TRUTH ABOUT INFERTILITY

Primary infertility (what people most often refer to) is defined as the inability to conceive after one year of unprotected intercourse or the inability to carry a pregnancy to term. Less commonly recognized is *secondary infertility*, which is the inability to conceive or carry a child to term after one or more live births. Either case can be the source of deep emotional pain and place significant strain on relationships—especially between husband and wife, and between a person and God.

---

1. See Deuteronomy 28:18 and Genesis 20:18. The only possible exception to infertility as a national judgment might be the case of David's wife Michal (2 Sam. 6:23), but it is unclear from the text whether God closed her womb or David merely chose never to be intimate with her again.

Infertility is shrouded by common myths that cause many infertile couples to feel alienated and to be misunderstood. Some assume that infertility is a woman's problem and the solution is merely to relax. In reality roughly 30 percent of infertility cases are due to purely female factors. Another 30 percent are due to male factors. A combination of male and female factors make up 35 percent of cases, and the remaining 5 percent of cases remain unexplained. This means that in 95 percent of all infertility cases there is a diagnosable medical reason for which *no* amount of relaxation will help.[2]

Many assume that the couples "must have a lot of fun trying." Infertility actually has the reverse effect on marital sexual intimacy: 43 percent of women and 31 percent of men reported having at least one symptom of sexual dysfunction.[3] Sexual difficulties for infertile couples are five times greater than for fertile couples. "Trying" again in the context of numerous unsuccessful attempts carries with it an immense amount of pressure, adding a difficult and painful component to the marriage bed. These facts are important to understand in order to minister effectively in this crisis.

Adoption is often offered as a solution to infertility, but this fails to understand the grief of infertility. While adoption does solve the unfulfilled desire to parent, it does not resolve other losses (such as the longing to see a little person who looks a bit like each parent, seeing *their* child on ultrasound, or feeling movement in the womb). In addition, the adoption process itself involves losses and can be emotionally and financially draining. Adoption is not a solution to infertility, nor is it even possible for all couples. It is expensive, takes a great deal of time, and some couples may legitimately decide that adoption is not for them. Usually it is a good option only after the couple has reached the "acceptance" stage of grieving over infertility.

Wives typically experience infertility very differently from the way their husbands do. Men are able to compartmentalize their thoughts and feelings about infertility and generally have less need to talk at

---

2. Statistics here and elsewhere have been gleaned from years of experience specializing in Ob/Gyn and Infertility. For more specifics on infertility, see William R. Cutrer and Sandra Glahn, *The Infertility Companion* (Grand Rapids: Zondervan, 2005).

3. American Society for Reproductive Medicine, www.ASRM.org, Patient Fact Sheet, revised 2008.

length about the process. Women, on the other hand, often process their grief verbally, talking for hours without ever feeling "finished." The wife's more global and interconnected thought process, along with the monthly cycling and the frequent conversations centered around children among her friends, make the diagnosis seemingly inescapable. Many experience a great sense of shame in addition to the feeling of loss regarding their infertility. God's current withholding of children from a woman can cast shadows of doubt about God's love for her.

Husbands or wives may blame themselves—perhaps God is punishing them for something in their past, or perhaps He is withholding children because, as they tell themselves, "Maybe I would be a terrible parent." Misconceptions regarding infertility often result in unwittingly hurtful suggestions or comments that only serve to leave the couple feeling further isolated and ashamed.

God's current withholding of children from a woman can cast shadows of doubt about God's love for her.

MEDICAL INTERVENTIONS AND BIOETHICAL IMPLICATIONS

Some Christians are firmly against any assisted reproductive technologies (ARTs), believing that medical intervention in human reproduction is "playing God" and that doctors who may not value human life will take huge risks in the process. While there are important ethical issues to think through in reference to reproductive technology, it is unwise to make blanket statements about all medical procedures. Due to the wide variety of available testing, each treatment should be evaluated individually through the grid of scriptural ethics. If godly Christians choose to use certain of these technologies, they need to do so wisely, in a way that honors the dignity of life, even at the one-celled stage. It is inconsistent to view medical intervention as legitimate for treating infections, diabetes, and cancer, and yet automatically disregard medical science for overcoming reproductive ailments. The truth that God is in control yet allows a couple to suffer with infertility does not mean that they must be passive or that it "must be God's will" for them not to have children. Fortunately, God has allowed those in the medical field to make incredible advances in treating infertility, enabling many couples to experience the joy of giving birth.

To describe the many different hormonal and surgical interventions for infertility lies outside the scope of this short chapter. However, if you are ministering to a couple who are seeking medical treatment for infertility, it will be beneficial for you to do further reading in this area so that you can appreciate the unique struggles they face (see "Additional Resources" at the end of the chapter). Suffice it to say here that many of the evaluations and treatments are stressful and uncomfortable, often compounding the pressure the couple feels when "trying." Some such treatments are expensive, and the process of deciding how far to go in treating infertility may raise stewardship issues as well as ethical ones.

MINISTRY TO INFERTILE COUPLES

Many of the suggestions for ministering to those in grief (see chapter 2) are applicable when ministering to couples struggling with infertility.

- Listen to them.
- Weep with them.
- Pray with them.
- Refrain from asking if they have prayed about it. (In my twenty-five years of medical practice, no Christian couple that I have treated had failed to pray fervently already.)
- Avoid encouraging couples to "just relax" or asking if they have considered adoption. These statements are patronizing and hurtful.
- If you have kids, don't offer to lend them yours! Don't joke that they must not "know how." Such remarks are simply ignorant.
- Be patient—this suffering can drag on for years.
- Don't allow your compassion to turn to contempt.
- Don't be surprised if they seem at times to obsess or overreact. As mentioned earlier, we find in Proverbs 30 that it is normal for a childless woman to feel unsatisfied. True soul satisfaction is found in the Lord. Your steady presence can communicate this truth.

- Recognize that men and women generally have different grief responses to infertility, and check in on how their marriage is bearing up under this burden. If they are struggling, let the couple know that this is a common reaction for couples in their situation. This can normalize their experience and may provide a greater sense of openness for working through this added pressure in their marriage.

Having a safe context for talking through emotions can be immensely helpful for the wife—whether that be in a support group, with trusted friends, or a caring counselor. Since there is typically such a significant discrepancy between the husband's and wife's needs to verbalize this experience, such outlets for her also can lessen pressure on the marriage.

- Churches can take small, practical steps to make their communities more sensitive for those struggling with infertility.
- Be aware that "family-centered" holidays, especially Christmas, Mother's Day, and Father's Day will be difficult.
- Know that rejoicing with others who have discovered they are pregnant can be hard.
- Consider sending a card on a day that may be difficult.
- Be mindful of these couples as you plan Mother's Day services. (Consider not having mothers stand up. Instead, present flowers to all the women or at least include these families in the pastoral prayer, along with those who have lost their mothers or who are estranged from their mothers.) This can be a most difficult day. The same applies for Father's Day.
- Include couples such as Priscilla and Aquila (whose children, if they had them, did not define their ministry) in examples of model families.
- Recognize that the profound experience of pain is normal in this crisis, yet encourage childless couples to respond in kindness and grace to others who are uninformed or thoughtless. When possible, these couples can educate those who appear teachable.

• Encourage couples with the truth that their pain may one day open doors of ministry to others—especially those who struggle with similar pain, whether believers or unbelievers.

ADDITIONAL RESOURCES

Aspire2 at www.aspire2.com.

Cutrer, William R., and Sandra Glahn. *The Infertility Companion.* Grand Rapids: Zondervan, 2005.

Cutrer, William R., and Sandra Glahn. *When Empty Arms Become a Heavy Burden.* Nashville: B&H, 1996.

Hannah's Prayer Ministries at www.hannah.org.

The International Council for Infertility Information Dissemination at www.inciid.com.

RESOLVE, Inc. at www.resolve.org.

PREGNANCY LOSS

There are about 4.4 million confirmed pregnancies in the United States every year, and 900,000 to 1 million of those end in pregnancy loss. If you include loss that occurs before a positive pregnancy test, estimates suggest that perhaps 40 percent of all conceptions miscarry.[1] This is a shocking percentage and reflects how every congregation will be impacted by early pregnancy loss (miscarriage). Pregnancy loss may be the first genuine crisis a young couple has to face together, and it highlights the different ways that men and women respond to loss.

The shock and disappointment of pregnancy loss can overwhelm the young couple who have planned to conceive and raise a family, experienced the joy of a positive test, shared the good news, and then discover the child has died. Depending on how far the pregnancy has progressed, a medical procedure called D&C (dilation and curettage), or even the induction of labor for a late-term fetal death, may be necessary. Suddenly, what was once a joyful expectation has become a tragedy.

MINISTRY TO THOSE WHO EXPERIENCE PREGNANCY LOSS

Wives often experience enormous emotional upheaval as hormones drastically fall as a result of the baby's death. So, in addition to the cramping, bleeding, and prospect of a surgical procedure, their moods may swing wildly and unpredictably.

Husbands, trying their best to love well, often act "strong" and stoic, suppressing emotion. Sadly, this is counterproductive. Most women are

---

1. HopeXchange, www.hopexchange.com (accessed November 2008).

deeply emotional about pregnancy loss and need to see that their husbands feel the pain of loss as well. Otherwise, such women feel isolated in their suffering. My suggestion for husbands is to listen intently as your wife repeats every word the doctor said, and every symptom she has felt or not felt. Then weep with her, weep for your child, and cling tightly to your spouse. Your presence and tender, nonsexual touch will communicate far more than words can.

From the ministerial standpoint, it is important to avoid compounding grief by saying insensitive things. To suggest that "there was probably something wrong with the pregnancy" offers no comfort. (The fact that perhaps as many as 75 percent of miscarriages do have chromosomal issues does not help the healing, especially at the beginning.) To suggest that the parents can always try again, or

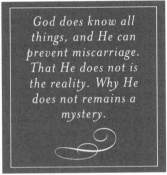

God does know all things, and He can prevent miscarriage. That He does not is the reality. Why He does not remains a mystery.

to say, "at least you conceived this time" again sounds patronizing, not edifying, and suggests that the child conceived is replaceable. To say, "It's for the best" and "God knew there was something about this pregnancy that wasn't right," only adds to the burden of loss. God does know all things, and He could have prevented the miscarriage. That He *did not* is the reality. *Why* He did not remains a mystery.

What, then, might you consider doing? Do show up. Do care. Do express your sorrow for the loss. (This *is* the genuine loss of a human life.) Human beings have eternal significance, whether they live a few days in the womb or one hundred years on the earth. God is sovereign, *and* the pain is real. These are not mutually exclusive concepts. One can fully trust God and still hurt, suffer the pain of loss, and weep. God knows all about suffering, and He will not leave or forsake this dear family in the midst of such a trial.

SECOND AND THIRD TRIMESTER LOSS: STILLBIRTH, FETAL DEMISE

When the pregnancy has progressed to the second or third trimester before the baby dies, the minister should expect very powerful grief reactions. This event, while relatively rare, usually occurs unexpectedly, without any symptoms to warn of the impending crisis. Women have enjoyed smooth pregnancies only to find at a routine office visit or scheduled sonogram evaluation that the baby has died. Sometimes the mother notices decreased and then absent fetal movement, but more often the news comes as a total surprise. Husbands may not even be present at that office visit and are often called by the doctor's staff to come immediately to assist in comforting the wife.

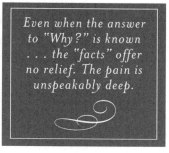

Even when the answer to "Why?" is known . . . the "facts" offer no relief. The pain is unspeakably deep.

When you as a minister become involved, remember the power of prayer and presence. No words can possibly soothe in such times. In fact, even when the answer to "Why?" is known (knot in the cord, placental problems, abnormal fetal development), the "facts" offer no relief. The pain is unspeakably deep. So, the answer to the "why" question is usually, "I really don't know."

It is almost always important that the mother plan to see the child and even hold the baby after the birth. Even babies who have been dead for an extended period of time or have major birth defects have areas of beauty that the medical staff can highlight. My experience tells me that the mother *does* need to see the infant to have closure and sure knowledge that the baby did die. For those rare exceptions, where the mother refuses to see the child or for medical reasons cannot, I recommend the staff take a few pictures and/or provide a lock of hair, because some weeks down the road, mothers and fathers find considerable comfort in these keepsakes.

Babies who reach the second trimester may weigh one-half pound to two pounds and will be fully formed when delivered. A memorial service and perhaps burial will be appropriate. State laws vary as to what is considered a "stillbirth" requiring funeral arrangements and what is considered a miscarriage where the fetus will be taken care

Grieving parents are at high risk for marital fracture. Marriages often do not survive the loss of a child in late pregnancy or early childhood.

of at the hospital. Sensitivity is essential here. Refrain from any talk about future pregnancies or encouragement that "it will all work out for the best." Just grieve the loss along with the grieving parents.

Presiding over such funerals is very difficult and will require considerable energy and compassion. Note that marriages often do not survive the loss of a child in the second trimester of pregnancy or in early childhood, so appreciate that this couple is "high risk" for marital fracture.

Strive to walk with the couple, not only through the process of the funeral but also in the months to come. Remembering the anniversary of the baby's "due date" and, of course, the death date with a call or a card makes an enormous impact. Be sure to consider your own emotional health during these crises as well, because bearing such burdens will exact a significant toll on you, the minister.

ADDITIONAL RESOURCES

Davis, Deborah. *Empty Cradle, Broken Heart*. Golden, CO: Fulcrum Publishing, 1996.

Hayford, Jack W. *I'll Hold You in Heaven*. Ventura, CA: Regal, 2003.

Heydrick, Debbie. *I'll Hold You in Heaven Remembrance Book*. Ventura, CA: Regal, 2003.

MacArthur, John. *Safe in the Arms of God: Truth from Heaven About the Death of a Child*. Nashville: Thomas Nelson, 2003.

SEXUAL ADDICTION

The fastest expanding area of crisis ministry these days concerns issues of sexual immorality in the church. Obviously, sexual sin is not new to the followers of Christ, but it represents a remarkable affront to the name of Jesus. Scripture clearly communicates that our sexuality (genetics, gender roles, and physical expression) is given by God as He created us male and female and blessed the race with the privilege of "being fruitful." God's design for sexual expression, as understood from brain structures and neurochemistry, included the pleasurable sensations that can tempt people to sexual sin. Every good gift God has given has the potential for abuse and misuse, and sexuality is certainly no exception.

Full sexual expression belongs within the confines of the marital covenant: one man with one woman for a lifetime. Yet sexual problems exist within marriages, premaritally, and extramaritally that require the minister to understand normal human sexuality, develop a level of comfort in discussing sexual issues, and confront sexual sin boldly.

A BIBLICAL APPROACH TO SEXUAL TEMPTATION

God created the human race with certain basic needs: air, water, food, and shelter. Rarely do we give any thought to the essential need for oxygen that our air provides, but without it we would die within a few minutes. For one gasping for air, the drive to survive is powerful. Similarly, without water, we would die in a matter of days. The strong desire for water—thirst—can overwhelm us and, unless it is satisfied, brain and body functions deteriorate rapidly. Without food or shelter, we can survive longer than we can without oxygen or water, depending on our "body fat" stores and the severity of the elements, but ultimately, we need nourishment.

Each of these needs has a corresponding desire that God has placed within us. The desire for survival and our bodies' necessities are part of our humanity. For each natural desire, however, there can be accompanying excesses and dangers. Excessive eating or drinking has a negative effect on the body. Even oxygen can be toxic at high concentrations for long periods of time. While sexual desire represents a strong natural drive, sexual expression is not a need in the same way as oxygen, food, or water. Our personal survival does not depend on a sexual outlet. Nonetheless, the drive can be particularly strong in many individuals; and while the desire is natural and holy, it can entice us to excess—to sin.

Our sexuality includes not only our genetically determined gender (XX or XY) but also the libido, the sex drive. This inborn desire for sexual interaction—to meet and connect intimately with another person physically—is part of God's design for us. Yet the God-given gift of sexuality comes with guidelines the Creator outlined for our spiritual and emotional health.

Temptation arises when we desire something that is unobtainable without committing sin. It is not a sin to be tempted; the sin comes in acting on a desire in a way that violates God's pattern for holy living. Gluttony and drunkenness are condemned in Scripture, as is sexual immorality. Thus, just as the desire for food is good but can be abused, the desire for sexual expression is good but can be misused. Adults are created to express themselves sexually, but we can each be tempted to pursue sexual gratification outside scriptural guidelines (limited to husband and wife in covenant marriage relationship).

God is relational and has created us for relationships. We long for connection with God and with one another. God's gift of sexuality has multiple purposes but only a single relationship for valid expression. Sex glorifies God, not only in the procreative act, but also as a way of intimate communication between husband and wife and mutual physical delight.[1] We must recognize that many couples suffer from sexual difficulties, so some might dispute whether sex is either good or a gift. In Song of Songs, however, Scripture indicates that the intimate

---

1. William Cutrer and Sandra Glahn, *Sexual Intimacy in Marriage* (Grand Rapids: Kregel, 2007).

physical pleasure derived from the experience is good and God-given. Interestingly, children are not even mentioned in Song of Songs.

Temptation in the area of sexuality represents a basic struggle for control over one's life. Is God sovereign? Will we humbly submit to His authority by obedience to His Word in the area of sexuality, or will we rebel and pridefully reject God's path?

Temptation in the area of sexuality represents a basic struggle for control over one's life.

What will we do when faced with sexual temptation? Will we yield to it? Will we linger in it and delight in it? Will we choose to pursue the object of temptation rather than God? Answering yes to any of these questions means sin. The desire for sexual gratification has superseded the longing for holiness. Sex has become the priority; sex has become an idol separating us from God.

Lust describes sexual desire burning out of control. It is so powerful that Scripture instructs us to flee (rather than stand and fight) from sexual immorality because this temptation is so strong that we will succumb otherwise (see 1 Cor. 6:18).

Consider the following Scriptures that provide hope for those who struggle with lust:

- God is faithful to forgive and cleanse us (1 John 1:9).
- God knew every day of our lives before we were born (Ps. 139:16).
- God loves us with unconditional (Eph. 1:4–8), inseparable (Rom. 8:35–39), and enduring love (John 10:28–29).
- We are engaged in a battle between flesh and Spirit (Rom. 7–8).
- If we draw near to God, He will draw near to us (James 4:8).

The struggle for sexual purity will be one of the central spiritual battlefields for now and the foreseeable future. Internet pornography alone is a multibillion-dollar per year industry. Graphic sexual images are available on television, on the Internet, in movies, and in magazines. Many are falling, even within the church. We must be prepared. We must be vigilant. We must invest time and prayerful attention to both prevention and restoration in the area of sexual sin.

THE DEFINITION OF SEXUAL ADDICTION

Except between consenting husband and wife, acting out one's sexual impulses is sin.

There now exists considerable research in the field of human sexuality, with experts writing from the Christian perspective as well as the secular. Willingham, in *Breaking Free*, defines sexual addiction as "an obsessive-compulsive relationship with a person, object or experience for the purpose of sexual gratification."[2] This definition is quite useful in that it broadly includes the spectrum of attachments that can tempt people into sexual sin.

As a physician, I am not enthusiastic about the term *sexual addiction*, because medically *addiction* carries powerful connotations about the symptoms of withdrawing from the substance of addiction. For example, an alcoholic who "quits" may experience dramatic physical symptoms of withdrawal, including hallucination, seizures, and even death. Likewise, narcotic addicts, if they stop abruptly, face overwhelming physical side effects.

Such is not the case for sex addiction. Though the individual may have a strong drive for gratification, the neurochemicals involved in sexual pleasure (endorphins, enkephalins, dopamine, oxytocin, and others) do not cause symptoms of withdrawal in the face of abstaining. Consequently, I view such a sexual problem as more closely akin to an obsessive-compulsive disorder. The vast weight of research and writing, however, has adopted the term *addiction*, so we will use it.

Some have denied that sex addiction is even a problem, suggesting that humans should act out their sexual impulses as long as they're within the law. Let me state clearly: except between consenting husband and wife, acting out one's sexual impulses is sin. The Bible gives guidelines permitting full sexual expression within marriage, but premarital sex, extramarital sex, and the use of pornographic materials for sexual excitation are contrary to holy living and pure thinking.

Mark Laaser, a Christian counselor and recovering sex addict, has written extensively in the area and notes that a sense of isolation and

---

2.   Russell Willingham, *Breaking Free* (Downers Grove, IL: InterVarsity Press, 1999), 27.

abandonment are common to "sex addicts." Various behaviors categorize the individuals struggling with sexual temptations. Some require legal remedy, but most individuals respond to what the church freely offers:

- The gospel of Jesus Christ
- Forgiveness of sins
- Empowerment by the Holy Spirit to walk worthy of God's high calling

THE STRUGGLE WITH SEXUAL ADDICTION

For those struggling with temptation and sexual sin, there seems to be no escape. There are feelings that "no one would love me if they really knew the truth." These are accompanied by the sense that these issues are so horrible that they could never be shared, so individuals try to solve the problem alone. The best long-term observational research demonstrates that without ongoing help, sexual addicts cannot free themselves and will ultimately return to their sexual sin.

Once discovered, or having confessed, the repentant brother or sister needs Christian accountability and encouragement to begin again to walk the path of holiness. This ever-growing group of sufferers needs the ongoing ministry of the crisis team. It will take time, ongoing confrontation, encouragement, and patience to see this through. Humans tend to like quick answers and instant solutions. Yet for the one struggling with sex addiction, the problem goes deep, to the very thoughts and heart of the individual, and thus requires lifelong relationships to deepen a love for Christ that overcomes the love for illicit sexual pleasure.

> *For the one struggling with sex addiction, the problem goes deep, to the very thoughts and heart of the individual, and thus requires lifelong relationships to deepen a love for Christ that overcomes the love for illicit sexual pleasure.*

Accountability is important and of great value, but accountability changes *behavior*; repentance alone can change the heart. True life change begins with transformation of the heart and goes beyond weekly meetings or daily phone calls. Confession, repentance, and restoration are foundational to meaningful and lasting character change.

The behaviors involved can range from pornography use and masturbation all the way through involvement with prostitution. Each struggler has his or her own pattern, from the first thought and fantasy to the behavior chosen. Believers have been caught up in these sinful lifestyles, including:

- exhibitionism (exposing themselves)
- voyeurism (observing others in sexual situations)
- froteurism (rubbing up against people in crowded situations for the purpose of self-gratification)
- pornography use

A person entangled in sexual sin may develop a "tolerance" to one type of activity and so progress to deeper perversions, including child molestation, incest, and/or rape. The pattern of sexual addiction is important to understand if you are going to be involved in helping someone struggling in this area.

The experts in this field have discovered a certain "cycle" of behavior that, when understood, can assist us in ministering to these people. This cycle generally begins with the thoughts (fantasy), which—triggered by sights, sounds, and smells—powerfully draw this person to *search* for sexual stimulation and gratification. Most addicts form their own "ritual" of behavior that ends with the acting out, which might be viewing porn, visiting a prostitute, flashing, or any of the myriad of behaviors mentioned. Once they are preoccupied with the thoughts, the cycle will run to conclusion—sinfully acting out—unless intervention occurs. So, those who wish to minister in this crisis must connect and intervene at the time the thought process begins. Once the individual begins to fantasize about sexually acting out, the process has begun, and unless the progression can be blocked, that person will once again find sexual gratification, which leads to momentary bliss, followed quickly by guilt (feeling badly about what one has done) and shame (feeling badly about who one is).

As mentioned, individuals struggling with sex addiction generally feel isolated and abandoned. Thus, they haven't experienced the true intimacy of ongoing Christian fellowship but have substituted a temporary fix, a quick high, a false intimacy. As ministers, we can share the love of Christ and the experience of a Godly, nonsexual intimacy that includes a sense of belonging and hope.

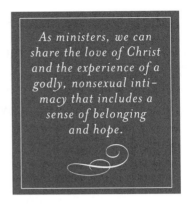

As ministers, we can share the love of Christ and the experience of a Godly, nonsexual intimacy that includes a sense of belonging and hope.

God's grace is sufficient for every need, and clearly grace is sufficient for this struggle. While these people feel totally out of control, unable to stop, God's grace and love can make the difference. Your presence, which includes a steady willingness to walk with them through this struggle, can be healing. Finding in you someone who loves them despite the sin that seems to control them can break the stronghold and open the possibility for change.

AT RISK FOR SEXUAL ADDICTION

The research suggests that both men and women who were emotionally abused as children (97%), sexually abused (81%), or physically abused (74%) are at risk for sexual addiction.[3] People who were exposed at an early age to sexually explicit material likewise face greater risk. Often individuals who are socially isolated, preferring to live as "loners," may be at risk for developing sexual problems.[4]

In summary, children who do not receive appropriate physical touch, love, nurture, and affirmation are more likely when they grow into adulthood to seek gratification in false-intimacy encounters. These factors alone make taking a good history of the family and early relationships essential and enlightening for those who would care for brothers and sisters in this crisis. These factors are not "excuses" for sinful behavior but merely the framework that puts people at risk. The power of the indwelling Holy Spirit strengthens each believer such that victory over sexual sin is truly possible.

---

3. Mark Laasar, *Faithful and True: Sexual Integrity in a Fallen World* (Grand Rapids: Zondervan, 1996), 101.

4. Douglas E. Rosenau, *A Celebration of Sex* (Nashville: Thomas Nelson, 2002), 362.

MINISTRY TO THOSE WITH SEXUAL ADDICTIONS

In the introduction, I discussed the intense intimacy that develops in crisis ministry. Sexual crisis ministry is a particularly intimate context. Again, be forewarned about the powerful emotions that can develop in you toward the person in need and vice versa. Surround yourself with others who have permission to ask you difficult questions about your motives. Be vigilant of well-set boundaries and stay accountable to others so that you do not abuse your position of respect and authority.

Ministry can be complex, and when sexual issues are in view, wisdom suggests that mature, trained men work with men and mature, trained women work with women. (Perhaps as many as 10 percent of sex addicts are women.) When dealing with a sex addict who is married, married ministry teams can be of great value. Couple counseling can be done along with individual work. Sex addiction often means different things to a man or a woman. Men are generally pursuing the erotic experience itself, whereas women often are pursuing relational intimacy via physical expression. Thus, a man is more likely to understand another man's struggle, a woman better able to connect with the woman who is struggling or the wife of the addict. Training in this sensitive area can be offered within the church separately or as part of training "marriage mentors" so couples have sufficient competency to recognize these problems and either help or refer. Occasionally legal issues arise, so access to competent counsel becomes a church ministry necessity.

ADDITIONAL RESOURCES

Arterburn, Stephen. *Every Man's Battle.* Colorado Springs: Waterbrook, 2000.

Cutrer, William, and Sandra Glahn. *Sexual Intimacy in Marriage.* Grand Rapids: Zondervan, 2007.

Elliot, Elisabeth. *Passion and Purity.* Grand Rapids: Revell, 2002.

Ethridge, Shannon, and Stephen Arterburn. *Every Woman's Battle.* Colorado Springs: Waterbrook, 2003.

Evans, Tony. *Sexual Purity.* Chicago: Moody Press, 1995.

Laaser, Mark. *Healing the Wounds of Sex Addiction.* Grand Rapids: Zondervan, 2004.

Willingham, Russell. *Breaking Free.* Downers Grove, IL: InterVarsity Press, 1999.

SEXUALLY TRANSMITTED DISEASES

Sexually transmitted diseases (STDs, or STIs—Sexually transmitted infections) have become a hidden epidemic. The Centers for Disease Control and Prevention (CDC) reports that five of the top ten leading infectious diseases are sexually transmitted.[1] Sex was never meant to make people sick, yet the practice of "casual" sex, outside the God-ordained boundaries of marriage, has proven dangerous and even deadly.

STDs are primarily contracted through sexual behavior—whether voluntary or involuntary—through exchange of bodily fluids. In a small percentage of cases, a person has contracted an STD through the blood, the birth process or breast milk, or an organ/tissue transplant.

STDs are either bacterial or viral. Most STDs caused by bacteria can be effectively treated with antibiotics; however, viral STDs cannot be cured with medication. Once a person contracts a viral STD, it poses a problem for life. Not only have STDs increased among teens and young adults, but STDs also have increased among those fifty years of age and older.

Scripture exhorts human beings, who are made in God's image, to remain pure in singleness and to remain faithful within marriage. God created us male and female, with different gender identities (Gen. 1:27). Therefore, sexual distinction is important to God. A person's body is a holy creation of God, specifically designed for a glorious purpose.

---

1. Centers for Disease Control and Prevention, www.cdc.gov, is a good resource for up-to-date information on health issues. Facts in this chapter are largely available from this source.

When a person becomes a follower of Jesus Christ, the Holy Spirit resides in his or her body—the body becomes the temple of the Holy Spirit (1 Cor. 6:19).

God's design for sexual intimacy is the union of one man and one woman in the God-created covenant of marriage for life (Gen. 1:28; 2:24–25).

Celibacy outside of marriage and the faithfulness of both partners within marriage are the lifestyles most certain to protect against STDs.

Outside of that covenant of marriage, everyone is to refrain from sexual activity in obedience to God, honoring Him with purity of body, mind, and soul.

God designed humanity to procreate through sexual intercourse. Therefore, joy in the midst of sexual intimacy is a blessing from God. Sexual intimacy in proper context glorifies God, unifies husband and wife, and satisfies each physically and emotionally. The spiritual unity within a marriage should be reinforced in the act of intercourse.

In the context of sexual sin, Proverbs 6:27 says, "Can a man hold fire against his chest without burning his clothes?" Sexual expression outside of marriage is sin and results in a variety of possible consequences. One such consequence is contracting an STD. While STDs *may* be transmitted through blood transfusions or the use of an infected needle, most often they result from sex. Therefore, celibacy outside of marriage and the faithfulness of both partners within marriage are the lifestyles most certain to protect against STDs.

FACTS ABOUT STDS

Today, there are more than twenty-five significant STDs (up from only two major STDs—syphilis and gonorrhea—prior to 1960). Over fifteen million Americans contract a new STD infection each year. Approximately two-thirds of all STD infections occur in people under twenty-five. Such diseases are not only painful, but some are life threatening as well. STDs are involved in certain cancers, fertility problems, brain dysfunctions, and even stillbirths.

• **Bacterial STDs.** As mentioned above, STDs are either bacterial or viral. The more common bacterial STDs are chlamydia, gonorrhea, and syphilis. These bacterial STDs can be treated and cured; however, some STDs have no obvious symptoms and can cause damage to the body before being diagnosed. For instance, 85 percent of women who have chlamydia show no signs of infection. This STD may be discovered during a woman's annual examination (if the gynecologist orders the appropriate test). Chlamydia damages the delicate mechanisms in a woman's fallopian tubes, which may render her infertile. Chlamydia is the most common nonviral STD (with four million new infections annually) and is a leading cause of infertility. Gonorrhea can lead to arthritis, infertility, and pelvic pain in females. Teens (ages 15–19) are infected with gonorrhea more than any other age group. This particular infection has developed resistance to most of the antibiotic therapies that have been used for decades.

• **Syphilis.** Syphilis is a bacterial STD that can be treated with high-dose penicillin if caught in time. Most people have no symptoms other than a painless ulcer that goes away on its own. However, after a period of time, the disease becomes systemic and can cause problems with multiple organ systems. Syphilis is the fifth most commonly reported infectious disease in America, as reported by the CDC in 2006.

• **HPV.** The number one viral STD in America is human papilloma virus (HPV), with more than 5.5 million new infections each year. HPV causes genital warts and is involved in more than 90 percent of cervical cancer cases. New cases of HPV are five times more common than all other STDs. HPV is passed on by moist skin to moist skin contact, so a condom will not fully protect against it. Although a multistage immunization shot may be given to young teens to protect against some strains of HPV, not all strains of HPV can be prevented. Currently a publicity campaign to vaccinate all women to "prevent cancer" does not even mention that what is truly prevented is a sexually transmitted infection. Those recommending this vaccine (Gardisil) assume that all young girls will be sexually promiscuous or connect with infected boys. Some experts suggest that a woman has an 80 percent risk of contracting HPV during her lifetime. Understanding these facts can assist in premarital counseling when one of the couple has had extensive premarital sexual experience. In these cases, the vaccine might well make sense. Refer her to her physician for appropriate evaluation and treatment.

STDs are essentially contracted through sexual behavior—either voluntary sexual activity (exchange of bodily fluids that could include kissing, genital-area touching, vaginal or anal intercourse, or oral sex), or through involuntary sexual activity (rape, incest). Other ways (percentages are low but still present) a person may contract an STD are through blood (needles/transfusions), the birth process, breast milk, (mother to infant), and organ/tissue transplant. When the genital warts caused by HPV appear, they can be treated by cryotherapy (freezing) or laser ablation (vaporizing), or dissolved with an acid solution, but they ordinarily return.

• **Herpes.** One in every five Americans over the age of twelve has genital herpes. Since genital herpes is a viral STD (distinct from HPV), the infected person will have herpes for the rest of his or her life, though it may manifest unpredictably. Many people are infected with herpes and yet have never had any symptoms. Common fever blisters (cold sores) are a type of herpes and can be passed during sexual activity. Herpes can be transmitted even when sores are not present, and outbreaks can occur at any time. Genital herpes causes blisters and ulcers in the genital area, which cause pain on contact and painful urination. Medicine can help minimize outbreaks but cannot prevent transmission of the STD.

• **HIV/AIDS.** More newspaper and television press since 1981 has been given to HIV (human immunodeficiency virus)—the virus that causes AIDS (acquired immune deficiency syndrome)—than any other STD. A 2006 report estimated that, in the United States, the cumulative number of deaths of persons with AIDS was 565,927, with approximately 450,000 people living with AIDS.[2]

---

2. Centers for Disease Control and Prevention, www.cdc.gov/hiv/topicssurveillance/resources/reports/2006report.

HIV can be passed on from the mother to the baby in the womb, though aggressive therapy can minimize this risk. Once HIV infected, most individuals will carry the infection throughout their lifetime.

The most common reaction to an STD diagnosis is denial. The shock of the news and its implications present a major crisis. Most feel afraid and alone. Some remain in denial and fail to do follow-up testing and treatment. Many do not alter their sexual behavior or even inform their "contacts," if there are several of them.

These diseases are more than warts, sores, and blisters. These diseases may continue for a lifetime and may actually be life threatening!

MINISTRY TO THOSE INFECTED WITH STDS

Premarital and extramarital sexual activity within the church has reached staggering proportions. Of particular note is the widespread practice of oral sex, even among church youth. Because there is no fear of pregnancy and many in prominent secular leadership have declared that "oral sex is not sex," young girls (ages 10 and up!) are experimenting with it in order to "belong" to their peer group or to keep a romantic relationship intact. This presents incredible dangers because girls this age do not have the maturity to handle such intimacy. My suspicion is that we will see a huge increase in sexual dysfunction in marriage when these girls grow into maturity and try to establish an appropriate intimacy with their husbands. I've found no current research on the long-term effects for girls or boys with such early sexualization other than the increased risk of sexual addiction/obsession (see chapter 7).

> *Appropriate steps must be taken to ensure the safety and privacy of the infected individual while providing a secure environment for family worship.*

Church leaders will have to face decisions about members infected with STDs, particularly with HIV/AIDS. Decisions about nursery arrangements for infected children and fellowship precautions within the church will become potentially divisive dilemmas. Nursery policies should include proper hand-washing technique and appropriate disposal of diapers and other material stained with bodily fluid. STDs (including HIV) do not "jump" from one crib to another or survive long on surfaces appropriately cleaned. Fear among other members of the church will have to be appreciated and appropriate steps taken to ensure the safety and privacy of the infected individual while providing a secure environment for family worship.

If the STD resulted from voluntary sexual intimacy (either as a single or with another person who is not the person's spouse), the person will likely feel fear, shame, and guilt. They may see their sin as unforgivable and its consequence as a sign of God's ongoing anger with them. Alternately, they may feel indignation, and have a hard time acknowledging the natural consequence of their sin. In either situation, the STD does not diminish a person's value as a human being created in God's image, nor does the STD eliminate the person's potential for future ministry.

Those infected need to know facts on how to combat the STD. We can encourage them to follow up and follow through with their physician. They will likely benefit from an accountability relationship to modify their sexual behavior. And we can guide them through repentance and confession so that they can find forgiveness and restoration in the Lord.

In the past, the age group of fifty-plus had a relatively low percentage of STDs. Due to a climbing divorce rate, the availability of male-enhancement drugs, and the fact that people are living longer in general good health, however, the STD rate for this age group has increased. Generally, women over fifty no longer need to use birth control devices. Invulnerable to pregnancy, they forget that they are still vulnerable to STDs. Many have lost their spouses and have returned to the dating scene, which has become progressively more accepting of sexual behavior that is contrary to Scripture. Thus, you can expect to minister to more people in this age group than in previous years.

Those who have contracted STDs in the act of rape or incest need special care. Grieve with them over the violence and violation they have experienced. They are innocent victims in need of comfort and reaffirmation. The perpetrators are the guilty parties, not them. Therefore, they need to refrain from punishing themselves for having the STD. Whether the STD is curable or only treatable, seeking medical treatment will be seeking the best for their bodies, minds, and souls.

SEXUALLY TRANSMITTED DISEASES

We have many sexually wounded members in the body of Christ. The spiritual leadership of the church must be informed and alert to the dangers facing their congregation, and this clearly includes sexual issues. Leaders need the confidence and competence to address these issues in a healthy, holy way. Sexuality is not a surprise to God. He designed it and entrusted us with it. We must be able to articulate clearly and boldly when issues like a general immunization program for a sexually transmitted infection (HPV) faces our communities and congregations so they can understand and decide biblically how to respond.

ADDITIONAL RESOURCES

Larimore, Walt, and Mike Yorkey. *The Highly Healthy Teen.* Grand Rapids: Zondervan, 2004.

Marr, Lisa. *Sexually Transmitted Diseases: A Physician Tells You What You Need to Know.* 2nd edition. Baltimore: Johns Hopkins University Press, 2007.

Messer, Donald E. *Breaking the Conspiracy of Silence: Christian Churches and the Global AIDS Crisis.* Minneapolis: Augsburg Fortress, 2003.

Why kNOw Abstinence Education Program at www.whyknow.org.

DIVORCE AND REMARRIAGE

Nearly 67 percent of marriages will end in divorce prior to reaching the fortieth anniversary. The divorce rate for second marriages is 10 percent higher. An unhappy marriage increases chances of serious illness by 35 percent and shortens one's life span by four years. Following divorce, 75 percent of women remarry and 83 percent of men remarry.[1] Divorce not only touches the lives of the marriage partners but also affects the children, extended family, friends, work relations, church family, and others who respected the married couple. Thus, considerable time and energy should be invested in marital health and/or healing by the church's ministry team.

There are different social, psychological, and theological explanations for divorce. Most marital research identifies incompatibility, immaturity, financial issues, or sexual problems as potentially fatal to marital success. The laws have softened over the years, making "no fault" the prevailing "reason" for divorce, so no particular reason at all may be required. While society has accepted divorce as an almost normal part of life, the church often has responded less than graciously, ostracizing the divorced and their families. With such a large percentage of the population having experienced divorce, the church must learn better both to help couples avoid this crisis and to minister reconciling grace to individuals who have experienced it. At times sin must be confronted and dealt with, including the use of formal church discipline. Often mistakes of years past need the forgiveness that comes in Christ and the opportunity to move ahead.

---

1. John Gottman and Nan Silver, *The Seven Principles for Making Marriage Work* (New York: Random House, 1999), 4–5.

BIBLICAL PERSPECTIVE
ON MARRIAGE AND DIVORCE

We must begin with a theological understanding of marriage before developing a biblical approach to divorce. This means understanding that God ordained marriage as a permanent covenant relationship between one man and one woman for a lifetime. Ideally, marriage flourishes until that day when death dissolves the covenant vow, freeing the other, should he or she desire, to marry in the Lord. Sin damages the intimate oneness of a godly marriage and may lead to divorce. Sexual sin may provide a biblical reason for divorce, but it does not require divorce. Repentance and reconciliation remains the higher goal, with God glorified in the process.

While God does not forbid divorce but allows it because of "hardness of heart," He does regulate the practice. We learn in Deuteronomy 24 the guidelines for a legal divorce in ancient Israel. It involved three distinct stages. First, there must be a verbal declaration, then a written decree, and then the wife must be "sent out" from the home (women were not permitted to divorce in this cultural context). This allowed her to legally remarry in a culture that provided no real opportunities for a wife dismissed by her husband. God hates divorce (Mal. 2:14–16), but He Himself gave Israel a divorce decree in response to her immoralities and hardness of heart (Isa. 50:1). So, while divorce is always occasioned by sin, divorce is not always "sinful," since God divorced Israel. It's important to note here that God did not divorce Israel in a fit of anger or as an act of revenge but as a final, just act when all attempts at resolution had been rebuffed in that generation.

The New Testament teachings of Christ suggest that divorce may be permissible for *porneia*, the broadest Greek term for sexual immorality. Again, divorce is not required or even recommended because of it, but sexual sin may so fracture the marital covenant bond that even believers cannot restore intimacy. Paul writes in his letter to the Corinthians that a believer whose unbelieving spouse deserts is "not bound" (1 Cor. 7:15). I take that to mean "not bound" to the marriage covenant and thus free to divorce and remarry in the Lord. Others suggest it means "not bound" to pursue the deserter, but that seems beyond the text in its context. The Bible is silent about causes of divorce in addition to sexual immorality or desertion by an unbelieving spouse. For reasons in addition to these, Paul exhorts the believer to remain single or remarry the original spouse (presuming the original spouse has not remarried and divorced again).

Scripture does not address domestic violence as a reason for divorce. Clearly, a spouse in danger of physical harm should be protected, isolated from the abuser, and counseled toward reconciliation. In the event that an abuser continues the violence against a spouse, formal church discipline should be undertaken with the goal of restoration but with the possibility of exclusion and treating the abuser as an unbeliever. Repentance and life change are still required.

For those who have remarried following an unbiblical divorce, Scripture would suggest the new marriage has the stain of sin. That is not to suggest, however, that repentance means dissolving the current marriage.

Neither divorce nor divorce followed by improper remarriage constitute the "unpardonable sin," but there should be a time of confession, repentance, forgiveness, and restoration. You will likely encounter this situation often in your crisis ministry. The grace of Christ is sufficient for these delicate situations. Divorced persons who have repented often can be used mightily of God in certain roles in the church.

BIBLICAL PERSPECTIVE ON REMARRIAGE

God created the covenant of marriage (Gen. 2:24) and holds this union in high esteem. Because of sin, God permitted and regulated divorce in Old Testament times (Deut. 24:1–4). Regarding the parameters of divorce, Jewish interpreters were divided between two schools of thought. The more conservative school permitted divorce for sexual immorality; the other allowed a broad interpretation of Deuteronomy that included divorce for any "displeasing" activity on the part of the wife. Three necessary steps included the following:

1. Declaring three times "I divorce you"
2. Giving a written certificate
3. Sending the wife from the house

This freed the woman from her covenant commitment and permitted remarriage.

In the New Testament, however, Jesus and Paul limited the parameters of divorce to sexual immorality and desertion by the nonbelieving spouse. Although there are multiple interpretations of the passages involved, most scholars agree that if divorce is biblically permissible, then remarriage to another believer is likewise acceptable.

If someone is married before coming to Christ, he or she should continue on and strive to make the marriage successful. Having an unbelieving spouse is not grounds for divorce. To the contrary, the Christian spouse is encouraged to live in peace with the unbelieving partner with the goal of winning the spouse to faith in Christ (1 Cor 7:12–16; 1 Peter 3).

Scripture in both Old and New Testaments permits remarriage. In Deuteronomy 24:4 remarriage is discussed and permitted with specific boundaries (e.g., the first husband is not allowed to remarry his former spouse if she had remarried and her second husband divorced her or died). Also, the New Testament assumes remarriage with certain parameters (Matt. 5:32; 19:9).

Remarriage after widowhood clearly was permissible in the New Testament church and is so today (Rom. 7:2–3). In fact, Paul counseled young widows to remarry "because their passions may lead them away from Christ and they will desire to marry" (1 Tim. 5:11). Further Paul wrote, "So I want younger women to marry, raise children, and manage a household, in order to give the adversary no opportunity to vilify us" (1 Tim. 5:14). He reminded the widows, however, that they must marry only a Christian (1 Cor. 7:39).

After divorce, one should not rush into another marriage but rather reexamine the failed marriage to understand what contributions one made to the dissolution of the union. After understanding these realities, the Christian should strategize how to improve future relationships. Most importantly, he or she should seek relational healing through God and same-gender friends. One should see the divorce recovery process as a time to seek God's forgiveness as appropriate and perhaps offer forgiveness to the ex-spouse.

In remarriage one should understand how to deal with the decisions, memories, and mistakes of previous relationships. For instance, it's important to recognize the high expectations the divorced person may have for the second marriage. It's also important to understand the "triangulation" issue—that the second marriage involves the ex-spouse (to a certain degree) and children from previous marriages. Unconsciously, some may still harbor subconscious anger about the ex and the entire divorce process. When marrying another person with children, the new marriage may take as long as three years for the "blended family" to feel like a true family.

MINISTRY TO THE DIVORCED AND REMARRIED

Marriages end in divorce for various reasons—incompatibility, immorality, infidelity, immaturity. Divorce doesn't happen overnight. Rather, it progresses in stages from the first considerations of separation to the point of legal representation. Divorce affects every part of an individual's life. Many opportunities to minister arise along this pathway.

Most people don't want a divorce; they just want the pain within the marital relationship to go away. In ministering to those whose marriages have ended, help them face the truth and permanence of the divorce. And help them deal with the roller coaster of emotions that may include denial, anger, guilt, and shame. If needed, help them seek forgiveness of both God and the former spouse. Help them grieve the loss of the marital rela-

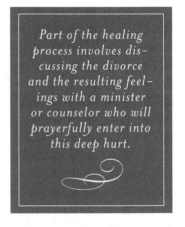

Part of the healing process involves discussing the divorce and the resulting feelings with a minister or counselor who will prayerfully enter into this deep hurt.

tionship. Part of the healing process involves discussing the divorce and the resulting feelings with a minister or counselor who will prayerfully enter into this deep hurt. God "heals the brokenhearted, and bandages their wounds" (Ps. 147:3).

If a person is at fault for the divorce, help him or her surrender the sin to the Lord and seek restoration in the Lord. If Jesus could see a future for the Samaritan woman, who had had numerous marriages and was now living in a sinful relationship, He can see a future for any repentant person. Divorce is *not* the unpardonable sin. God even blessed the Samaritan woman by letting her witness to others and seeing them turn to faith in Christ (John 4:39).

If the person was not responsible for the divorce, help him or her surrender the hurt, pain, and injustice to the Lord. Let Him work in the ex-spouse's life while the injured spouse remains devoted to the Lord and seeks God's wisdom, comfort, and strength. Help the injured person recognize the emotional upheaval that may characterize each day. This is normal for a time.

Children of divorce suffer as well. They may need help in seeing God's care and control through all of the pain, confusion, and insecurity. Most children blame themselves for their parents' divorces and wonder what they could have done differently or what they could do now to restore things to the way they were. You can help the children understand that they were not at fault and help them transition to a new family setting. As previously discussed, remarriage after divorce is permissible in certain circumstances, so help the children adjust to the changes they are facing.

In all of these situations, a personal commitment to pray for those who are divorced or are contemplating remarriage is crucial. They

A personal commitment to pray for those who are divorced or are contemplating remarriage is crucial.

need to know that someone cares about them and their future. They need to see a future filled with hope, even amid the consequences of divorce. Your ministry of faithful presence and gentle listening lets them know they are not alone in their suffering, regardless of the factors that led to the divorce. Again, they must be reminded that they are valued creations made in God's image. They need to see that God still has a plan for their lives. Remind them regularly of God's love for them. Also, as you minister consider your role as a blessing from the Lord as He told us in Galatians 6:2: "Carry one another's burdens, and in this way you will fulfill the law of Christ."

THE CHURCH'S ROLE IN DIVORCE PREVENTION

Extensive marital research has clarified some warning signs for marriages in trouble.[2] Research has identified "withdrawal" or "stonewalling"

2. I'm thinking specifically of the work done by John and Julie Gottman at the Gottman Institute

as a key sign of marital distress. This involves one partner disengaging from meaningful conversation, allowing the spouse to feel insignificant and his or her ideas unimportant. Marriages in which small disagreements escalate into major battles without any means of defusing the situation likewise have a high risk of failure. A contemptuous attitude toward the partner, excessive criticism, and an underlying belligerence—always looking for a fight—emerge from these secular researchers' studies as foreboding behaviors.

Compassionate involvement in the lives of people opens the door to ministry. Once the church becomes aware of marital distress, and even beforehand, steps can be planned to assist the marriages in the congregation. Biblical preaching constitutes the first line of defense against divorce by clearly com-

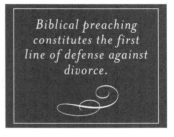

Biblical preaching constitutes the first line of defense against divorce.

municating what marriage is, what a covenant before God represents, and the responsibilities within that covenant. Nearly all divorces stem from personal sins, especially the prideful decisions that run contrary to clear biblical teaching. Thus, solid biblical preaching on marriage and what God desires in a home is foundational. Honestly addressing sin, repentance, forgiveness, and personal holiness from the pulpit helps people understand the sanctity of Christian marriage. In addition, preaching directly on the topic of divorce can help people think biblically when the idea first arises, before it has time to take root.

Premarital counseling also can be useful in preventing divorce. Churches should adopt a policy of not performing wedding services for any couple that has not successfully completed some form of premarital training (see chapter 16). Whether this is individual counseling, appointments with couples, or small groups of engaged couples, the emphasis on healthy marriage demonstrates a commitment by the staff to honor God in marriage. The premarital counseling should help couples to

---

(John M. Gottman and Nan Silver, *The Seven Principles for Making Marriage Work* [New York: Three Rivers Press, 2000]; see www.gottman.com) and by Howard Markman and Scott Stanley at the Center for Marital and Family Studies (Howard J. Markman, Scott Stanley, and Susan Blumberg, *Fighting for Your Marriage* [San Francisco: Jossey-Bass, 2001]; see www .du.edu/psychology/marriage).

understand each other better, know more about what to expect in marriage, and learn more about marital communication skills.

Marriage enrichment conferences, retreats, and/or messages also can strengthen the marriages in the church. Bad habits are easy to develop; outside expertise and encouragement are often required as couples learn to communicate, collaborate, and mature as one.

Finally, the pastoral staff and leadership should model healthy marriage habits in their own homes. Marriages that focus on God and on holiness, not merely temporal happiness, preach most effectively. Plus, an openness to marital counseling and referral to such counseling provide a proactive approach to marital health.

ADDITIONAL RESOURCES

Cutrer, William R., and Sandra Glahn. *Sexual Intimacy in Marriage.* Grand Rapids: Zondervan, 2007.

Adams, Jay E. *Marriage, Divorce, and Remarriage in the Bible.* Grand Rapids: Zondervan, 1986.

Akin, Daniel. *God on Sex.* Nashville: B&H, 2003.

Gottman, John M., and Nan Silver. *The Seven Principles for Making Marriage Work.* New York: Three Rivers Press, 2000.

Markman, Howard J., Scott Stanley, and Susan Blumberg. *Fighting for Your Marriage.* San Francisco: Jossey-Bass, 2001.

Rainey, Dennis. *Ministering to Twenty-first Century Families.* Nashville: Nelson Reference & Electronic, 2001.

Rosenau, Douglas E. *A Celebration of Sex.* Nashville: Thomas Nelson, 2002.

Smith, Harold Ivan. *A Time for Healing: Coming to Terms with Your Divorce.* Nashville: Lifeway Press, 2001.

DOMESTIC VIOLENCE AND SEXUAL ASSAULT

According to the U.S. Department of Justice, between 1998 and 2002, of the almost 3.5 million violent crimes committed against family members, 49 percent of these were crimes against spouses. They found that 84 percent of spouse abuse victims were female and 86 percent of victims of dating partner abuse were female. This study also showed that 50 percent of offenders in state prison for spousal abuse had killed their victims.[1] Approximately one in five female high school students reports being physically and or sexually abused by a dating partner.[2] In addition to reports of domestic violence, we see the startling figures on sexual assault, which indicate that 25 percent of eighth and ninth graders indicated that they had been victims of dating violence, including 8 percent who disclosed being sexually abused.[3] It is not limited to junior high and high school, however. Twenty-eight percent of victims are raped by husbands or boyfriends, while 35 percent are assaulted by acquaintances. Additionally, one of every six women has been the victim of rape or attempted rape in her lifetime. As staggering as these figures are, they

---

1. Matthew R. Durose, Caroline Wolf Harlow, Patrick A. Langan et al., "Family Violence Statistics," U.S. Department of Justice, Bureau of Justice Statistics, NCJ 207846, June 2005, http://www.ojp.usdoj.gov/bjs/pub/pdf/fvs.pdf.

2. Jay G. Silverman, Anita Raj, Lorelei A. Mucci, and Jeanne E. Hathaway, "Dating Violence Against Adolescent Girls and Associated Substance Use, Unhealthy Weight Control, Sexual Risk Behavior, Pregnancy, and Suicidality," *Journal of the American Medical Association* 286, no. 5 (2001): 572–79, jama.ama-assn.org/cgi/reprint/286/5/572.pdf.

3. V. A. Foshee, G. F. Linder, K. E. Bauman et al., "The Safe Dates Project: Theoretical Basis, Evaluation Design, and Selected Baseline Findings," *American Journal of Preventive Medicine* 12, no. 2 (1996): 39.

might actually be low, since the FBI estimates that nine out of ten rapes go unreported. Although 90 percent of rape victims are women, it might be surprising to learn that 3 percent of American men (2.78 million) have experienced a rape or attempted rape.[4]

The scope of such crimes staggers the imagination.

THE DYNAMICS OF DOMESTIC VIOLENCE

There is a unique dynamic to domestic violence. No one who enters into a relationship expects violence to develop, but where it does we can invariably trace a cycle that is set in motion and gradually climaxes in a violent act or acts. The first stage is the *romantic stage*, which might in fact be a phase of serene calm. However, this phase is followed by a *tension* that builds, resulting in a phase of *fear* of what might be coming. The initial abuse probably will be verbal or emotional, but ultimately a violent physical act occurs. There may or may not be a police report or an arrest, but regardless of police involvement, the next stage will be one of *remorse* in which the perpetrator vows to do better, begging (and usually receiving) forgiveness. Once forgiveness is offered and received with a renewed *vow to end the violence*, the cycle will unfortunately begin again with a *romantic stage* of variable length, *tension*, and so on.

Why do the victims go back? The reasons are varied. Some stay because of their Christian convictions, others because of the children. Many report having nowhere else to go. Abusive husbands can be very charismatic and even leaders in their churches. Other hindrances to escape include lack of money, lack of education to secure a job, mutual friends, family pressure, substance abuse, and the strongest hindrance of them all—*love*. Ultimately, domestic abuse is all about *control*. He abuses again and again because he can, and he can because she stays. Although many abusers are completely antisocial, many function very well in society; thus, friends or neighbors will say after the violence becomes public, "He was such a model husband" or "She was such a nice neighbor."[5]

Domestic violence presents many varied pictures. The target of the

4. University of Louisville, Health Sciences Center, Continuing Health Sciences Education, Domestic Violence online course, www.chse.louisville.edu/dviolencecourse.html (accessed 2007).

5. Patricia D. Fosarelli, *Family Ministry Desk Reference* (Louisville, KY: Westminster John Knox Press, 2003), 110.

abuse can be either the marriage partner, one or more of the children, or even an elderly family member. Forms of abuse are varied as well and include physical, sexual, and emotional/psychological abuse. Victims can also develop post-traumatic stress disorder, resulting in a variety of physical complaints, a general inability to concentrate, and even depression.[6] In search of an escape, victims may turn to alcohol or drugs. Additionally, children who witness violence in the home can bear emotional scars for the remainder of their lives. They may even grow into abusers themselves. In a national survey of more than six thousand American families, 50 percent of the men who frequently assaulted their wives also frequently abused their children.[7] More than fifteen million U.S. children live in families in which partner violence occurred at least once in the past year and seven million children live in families in which severe partner violence occurred.[8]

Many clues can serve as red flags to interested friends or relatives, alerting them to the violence occurring. Repeated visits to the emergency room or injuries that are hard to explain might serve as indicators. Even a delay in seeking treatment for unusual injuries can suggest violence in the home. The presence of a dominating or hovering partner during a doctor visit or your visit as a minister can suggest violence, since victims are reluctant to share what has happened with the perpetrator in the room. Also, too many people have preconceived notions of what violent homes look like, thinking that such homes must be from a certain socioeconomic group. Sometimes those close to the victim either do not believe what has been reported or they fear for their own safety and choose to remain uninvolved.

CHILD ABUSE

Abuse directed toward children cuts across social, educational, religious, ethnic, and racial boundaries. Poverty, social isolation, and

---

6.   Ibid.,109.

7.   Murray A. Strauss, Richard J.Gelles, and Christine Smith, *Physical Violence in American Families: Risk Factors and Adaptations to Violence in 8,145 Families* (New Brunswick: Transaction Publishers, 1990), 407–9.

8.   Renee MacDonald, Ernest N. Jouriles, Suhasini Ramisetty-Mikler et al., "Estimating the Number of American Children Living in Partner-Violent Families," *Journal of Family Psychology* 20(1): 137–42 (2006).

family disruption, however, are often prominent factors. Child abuse takes various forms: 60.5 percent of cases involve neglect; 18.6 percent are physical in nature; just under 10 percent of cases are sexual abuse; and 6.5 percent are emotional/psychological in nature. It is staggering to realize that between one and two thousand children die as a result of maltreatment yearly, of which 80 percent are under the age of five (and 40 percent of those are under the age of one year). Boys and girls are abused at nearly equivalent rates. Victimization rates decline as age increases, indicating that the most likely victims are the most helpless children.[9]

The primary perpetrators of child abuse are the victims' mothers acting as sole agents of the abuse (40 percent of cases). In 19 percent of cases, the fathers are the sole abusers, while in 18 percent of cases, the parents act together. Eleven percent of child abuse cases are perpetrated by a nonparental figure.[10] The thought that parents would abuse their own children seems inconceivable to most people. However, the excuses for the criminal behavior are varied:

- unwanted pregnancy
- premature birth
- child of undesired gender
- hyperactive child
- physically or mentally challenged child
- colicky child or one with other feeding/sleeping problems

The consequences of child abuse are serious. Children who witness abuse are six times more likely to attempt suicide and are 74 percent more likely to commit violent crimes, compared to children who are not abused. Abused children are more likely to fall victim to substance abuse, and they are significantly more likely to commit rape. Even if they do not commit violent crimes themselves, they are more likely to

9. Child Welfare League of America, http://www.cwla.org/programs/childprotection/child protectionfaq.htm#2002. See also, The Center for Women and Families, www.thecenter online.org.

10. U.S. Department of Health and Human Services, Administration for Children and Families, Child Maltreatment 2005. Washington, DC: U.S. Government Printing Office, 2007, http://www.acf.hhs.gov/programs/cb/pubs/cm05/chapterthree.htm#perp.

have trouble with interpersonal relationships, suffer from language disorders, and exhibit depressive symptoms.

GUIDELINES FOR MINISTRY

Detection of domestic violence can be difficult because the victims are frequently reluctant to share what is occurring, either because of fear of retaliation or because they are too embarrassed. It is essential for those who do make a discovery of domestic violence to realize that the violence is rarely a single event. It generally occurs over an extended period. You should enlist aid with spousal or elder abuse, which may include pastoral leadership and/or local agencies that specialize in this area. Detection in adults may be difficult because the victim minimizes or even denies what is happening at

IMPORTANT
CAVEAT:
You should enlist aid with spousal or elder abuse. . . . You must report suspected child abuse!

home. Also, the adult victim often feels responsible in some way. Many victims even fear that they might turn on their aggressor and kill their attacker. Even in the church when an individual seeking counsel seems to be hiding something, the minister—having established trust—can ask probing questions to provide an opportunity for revelation of what is happening at home:

- Are you here because of past or current injuries from your partner (or husband or caregiver)?
- Have you ever sought medical care because of abuse or threats from your partner (or caregiver)?
- You mentioned your partner is jealous (or loses control). Can you tell me more about that?
- What happens when your partner (or caregiver) loses control? What does that look like?

Detection in children is difficult because of their silence. You *must* report suspected child abuse! Signs to look for include sleep disturbances, bed-wetting, developmentally inconsistent behavior, or impaired inter-personal relationships. In counseling with children, it is important to establish rapport and clarify the goal, which is to understand the symp-toms or injuries. The counselor must remember to give age-appropriate explanation of what is going to happen. Patience is required, along with moving at a slow pace. The child must be reassured about his/her safety, but the child especially needs to be told that he/she is not to blame.

There are numerous ways a church may meet the physical needs of victims of domestic violence. In many cases, the appropriate response from a church counselor might include temporary change in residence for the sake of safety. Emergency shelter or transitional housing should be ready at a moment's notice. At times gracious church members might provide this service as well. Some churches may actually offer therapy and counseling opportunities, or the pastor might direct the victim to such services in the local community. Churches can, however, pro-vide support groups and emergency walk-in crisis counseling. In many cases medical/hospital and legal advocacy are needed.

SCRIPTURE TO COMFORT THE HURTING

Domestic violence can raise serious spiritual challenges for the vic-tim, who might very well ask, "Doesn't God care that my husband is beating me? Why doesn't He rescue me from this torture?" A child might cry out, "Why does God let Daddy hurt my mommy?" or simply "God, please make it stop." Yet the beatings do not cease. How does one address such painful questions? Your compassionate presence and wise use of Scripture can begin to bring comfort to those who are hurting.

As Psalm 9:9 states, "The LORD provides safety for the oppressed; he provides safety in times of trouble." There is comfort in that verse with-out indicating how or when God will act in the situation. God *is* our deliverer. Jeremiah 23:24 reminds believers that God does indeed know what is happening in every life, and He is all-powerful. Jesus reminded the woman at the well that He knew all of her life, and later in the same gospel, He reminded the disciples, "In me you may have peace. In the world you have trouble and suffering, but take courage—I have con-quered the world" (John 16:33).

Domestic violence can bring horrific pain and grief into a home.

Churches must provide the victims with physical help, such as financial assistance, home health care, legal advice, social services, and professional counseling. Simply put, victims need safety, security, hope, and people who believe them. Rather than ask, "Why does she stay?" consider reflecting on "Why does he beat her?" and begin a process of confronting the abuser for this sin. In my opinion, abuse—be it against a child, a spouse, or an elderly person—requires the steps of church discipline outlined in Matthew 18:15–17, beginning with a personal confrontation with a spiritual leader (see chapter 18 of this book). The goal of such discipline is reconciliation, but initially safety issues may well take precedence. These steps will require courage and reliance on the Lord and His Word, particularly in those situations that demand reporting the case to the proper authorities. Pastoral privilege and confidentiality do not extend to child abuse or suspected child abuse.

ADDITIONAL RESOURCES

Childhelp National Child Abuse Hotline: 800-422-4453.

Gargiulo, M. *Wings Like a Dove: Healing for the Abused Christian Woman*, VHS. Center for the Prevention of Sexual and Domestic Violence, 1997.

McDill, S. R., and Linda McDill. *Dangerous Marriage: Breaking the Cycle of Domestic Violence*. Toronto: Spire, 1998.

National Domestic Violence Hotline: 800-799-7233.

Tracy, Steven. *Mending the Soul*. Grand Rapids: Zondervan, 2005.

11
SEXUAL ABUSE

Sexual abuse is a much more rampant problem in our culture than many people realize. As the news media have exposed, many children are abused in the church itself by adults who misuse spiritual trust and authority. The problem of sexual abuse will likely worsen as sexual mores continue to deteriorate and as graphic sexual material becomes more readily available through the Internet and other sources. Early and frequent exposure to pornographic images distorts one's thinking toward sexuality and sexual expression.

As this problem continues to gain greater public attention, doubtless more victims will emerge who are willing to talk about their pain and seek help. While studying this issue is difficult because of the sometimes graphic and horrific nature of the material, the minister must face the harsh reality that such things happen in a fallen world and learn to help victims find healing in Christ.

Because of the intensely personal nature of sexual abuse, it is difficult to gain objective statistical data on this problem. Studies have shown that roughly 25 percent of adult women in this country were sexually abused as children; some suggest as many as 50 percent have experienced unwanted sexual touch. In the vast majority of cases of childhood sexual abuse, the offender is someone the child knows. Often the offender is someone who lives in the child's home. While most victims of abuse are girls, significant numbers of boys are abused as well. And while most offenders are male, some are female. Finally, it must be observed that abuse happens in every strata of society, even in the church. (See chapter 17 for guidelines on establishing a child protection policy for your church.)

Ministers must
be proactive
advocates for the
victimized.

There are a few general tenets to remember. The child is *never* at fault. Young children do not have the maturity to seduce and entice without prior exposure to sexually charged activity. However, since the children may experience pleasurable sensations during the contact, they often experience guilt feelings. To the abuser, secrecy is paramount, and various means of manipulation, including threats, are employed. Sexual abuse is a sin and a crime. Ministers must be proactive advocates for the victimized.

PSYCHOLOGICAL EFFECTS

The mental and emotional effects of sexual abuse tend to be long-term and can be quite severe, including intense shame and guilt, anxiety, relational problems, sexual dysfunction, and difficulty with trust and authority. Of course, the actual effects are unique to each individual and can include other issues such as an increased vulnerability to substance abuse and eating disorders, which present opportunities for victims to regain and exercise "control" over their bodies in at least one way. Some cut themselves to exert control, and through the pain they report some sense of relief.

When younger children experience themselves as helpless, shameful, and without power, they begin to believe this of themselves and act accordingly. When the victim has an ongoing relationship with the offender, as is usually the case, the sense of shame and unworthiness is repeatedly ingrained in the child. This is particularly true when the abuser shows kindness or favor to his victim, which happens in many cases. Shame leads to denial and/or silence on the part of the victim in many instances, leading to years of secret suffering. Such exploitation often has a devastating effect on future relationships, marriage, and parenting.

Teenagers who were abused as children often feel marginalized and begin associating with other disconnected, troubled teens. Thus, many wind up engaging in antisocial and delinquent behavior. Be aware of this when youth groups experience disruption centering on one particular individual.

SPIRITUAL EFFECTS

Sexual abuse has a profound spiritual impact on the child and the adult survivor. While many secular therapists ignore this aspect of abuse altogether, it is obviously of crucial importance in dealing with these issues from a Christian perspective. In my pastoral experience, I noted that individuals who had a history of abuse had difficulty with the image of God as "heavenly Father." Trust and faith issues often emerge if churches were involved in the abuse or ignored pleas for help.

There are several reasons for disillusionment with God and church in the wake of sexual abuse. One of these is the apparent contradiction that occurs between what the child is taught regarding God— that He loves children, cares for them, protects them—and the actual life experience of this child. Many survivors question where God was when these terrible things were happening to them. If God is really all-knowing and all-powerful, how could He allow them to be victimized in this way? Having had these thoughts, many victims feel betrayed by God and angry with Him, or they come to blame themselves and take responsibility personally for the perpetrator's crime. As a result, they feel betrayed, angry, and unable to trust or love this God. Such attitudes may even lead to a compounded sense of guilt in the survivor, who consequently feels far from God and/or unable to experience Him in a deep way.

MINISTRY TO VICTIMS OF ABUSE

One of the tragedies in sexual abuse is that when the victim gathers the courage to tell someone, whether a parent or church worker, the victim often is not believed. Many people simply do not want to accept that someone they know, and may even respect or love, could be capable of such grievous wrongs. Such people are in denial. Children do not lie about the abuse as a general rule, though they often lie to protect the abuser or family members he has threatened.

There should not be undue pressure too soon for the victim to forgive the perpetrator.

Much of the literature on the subject urges counselors and ministers alike, upon hearing a child's profession of abuse, to first and foremost believe the child and affirm him or her. Denial from adults is itself abusive, as it disrespects the child and indirectly supports the abuser.

Religious faith can have a positive influence in the healing process. Once the gospel can be clearly applied to the situation, the victim can experience the reality of a loving Father and can even forgive the offender. However, there should not be undue pressure too soon to forgive the perpetrator. Of particular importance to many victims is the emotional support that comes from establishing relationships with other women (or other men), and a relationship with God wherein they can pray and find true love and acceptance. The capacity to forgive often emerges slowly from this understanding that they were the victims but they are now free. When they can talk, share their pain, pray, and support each other spiritually, healing begins.

Sadly, some church ministries minimize these issues by simply telling the victim of abuse to forgive and forget. (This is particularly the case when the abuse has happened within the church itself.) Yet pressuring victims to simply forgive the abuser actually applies greater pressure to the victim and can reinforce feelings of guilt when he or she naturally finds forgiveness difficult.

Steven Tracy convincingly argues that there are three different types of forgiveness: judicial, psychological, and relational. *Judicial* forgiveness is God's granting forgiveness to repentant sinners through Christ's atonement. This, God alone can give. *Psychological* forgiveness takes place within the victim and involves "letting go of settled bitterness and rage, as well as committing the abuser to God, who is both loving and just." In psychological forgiveness, the victim gives up the right to seek revenge but trusts in the justice of God to deal with the sins that have been committed. *Relational* forgiveness involves reconciliation and restoration of relationship. This final type of forgiveness is always the goal, but it is often very difficult in cases of sexual abuse. Relational forgiveness, like God's judicial forgiveness, must be preceded by genuine repentance on the part of the offender. Tracy also points out that discretion is needed in considering repentance, as abusers are often very adept at manipulating words and actions to protect themselves and get their way. Precaution must be taken before relational forgiveness is granted to ensure that the repentance is genuine and lasting.[1]

Counselors need to be sensitive in helping victims forgive. Premature forgiveness, as many often urge, fails to deal with the deeper issues involved in both the victim and the perpetrator. In fact, premature forgiveness can be seen as abusive to the victim in minimizing the seriousness of what has happened; it encourages them to "let go" without ever engaging in a real process of healing from these very deep wounds.

In dealing with repentance and forgiveness, particularly in terms of relational forgiveness, it is crucial to identify appropriate boundaries, as set by the victim, within which this process can take place. This is important both because of the practical need to protect the victim from further trauma (physical and psychological), and because in the abuse itself, the victim's boundaries were invaded and he or she was made powerless.

Ultimately, the horrors of childhood abuse can be dealt with if treated sensitively. There is healing to be found, and that healing is found in Christ, for in Christ, God demonstrates that He values broken and hurting people so much that He Himself was hurt and broken in order to bring them into relationship with Himself. The minister can help these victims find the dignity that is theirs as people who are created in and bear the image of the God who made them. They can find hope in the promise that one day sin will be judged and all of creation will be made new through Christ. With patience, prayer, and practical help, victims can be made whole again.

IMPORTANT CAVEAT: *Sexual abuse of a child must be reported.*

Here are some steps you can take in ministering to victims of sexual abuse:

1. Listen well to the events as the victim describes them.
2. Allow the discussion to take sufficient time to come to completion.

---

1. Steven Tracy, *Mending the Soul* (Grand Rapids: Zondervan, 2005), 180–90.

3. Surround these visits and the victim with prayer.
4. Affirm the victim as one who was taken advantage of by someone in power/authority, and begin to outline the path to recovery. Likely this will involve individual appointments and group work as well.
5. As the victim heals, the issue of forgiving the abuser may be raised. However, there are legal matters to be considered. Sexual abuse of a child *must* be reported to the local child protective agency. Every church leader should know who to call in their community. The legal system can be involved to various degrees, depending on the desires of the victim, and this in itself is empowering.
6. Church discipline may well be appropriate if the perpetrator is a member or attender.

ADDITIONAL RESOURCES

Allender, Dan, *The Wounded Heart: Hope for Adult Victims of Childhood Sexual Abuse.* Colorado Springs: NavPress, 1995.

Heitritter and Vought, *Helping Victims of Sexual Abuse: A Sensitive Biblical Guide for Counselors, Victims and Families.* Grand Rapids: Bethany House, 2006.

Langberg, Diane, *Counseling Survivors of Sexual Abuse.* Longwood, FL: Xulon Press, 2003.

Rape, Abuse, and Incest National Network at www.RAINN.org; National Sexual Assault Hotline: 800-656-4673.

EATING DISORDERS

Crisis ministry can take many forms and sometimes presents itself quite unexpectedly. Eating disorders are potentially *fatal* problems affecting an enormous number of our young people. Data collected by Hoek and van Hoeken revealed a rise in incidence of anorexia in young women aged fifteen to nineteen in each decade since 1930. The incidence of bulimia tripled between 1988 and 1993. Only one-third of people struggling with anorexia receive mental health care.[1] In America, prevalence estimates for eating disorders in 2005 reached ten million.[2] Because of the potential danger in failing to appreciate the magnitude of this problem, this chapter has been devoted to this growing problem.

ANOREXIA

Anorexia (*anorexia nervosa*) is characterized by a preoccupation with dieting and "thinness" as a body image. While our society exalts the superslender model build, anorexics go way beyond even this, to excessive, dangerous weight loss. They experience a genuine fear of fat and gaining weight. When they look into a mirror, even when they are emaciated with almost zero body fat, they still see their body shape as obese. The sufferer does not recognize the seriousness of this problem!

Ninety percent of anorexics are women, but that means some young men suffer as well.[3] Though they are thin, they are excessively dieting

---

1. H. Hoek and D. van Hoeken, "Review of Prevalence and Incidence of Eating Disorders," *International Journal of Eating Disorders* 34 (2003): 383–96.

2. www.nationaleatingdisorders.org (accessed Jan 2009).

3. National Institute of Mental Health, http://www.nimh.nih.gov/health/publications/the -numbers-count-mental-disorders-in-america.shtml#Eating.

111

and/or exercising because they fear fat and food. One relatively early symptom of a serious problem in females is the loss of normal hormonal cyclicity (irregular periods).

A disorder with related traits is body dysmorphic disorder, an excessive concern over body shape, size, and weight. Both men and women suffer from this. Perception of body image becomes an obsession.

The news media constantly bombard us with the frightening data of how overweight Americans are. While this is undeniable, we must consider the fallout of that campaign. For some individuals, the onslaught of such negative information makes them feel unacceptable or worthless if their body image doesn't match the "norm." More than half of adult Americans are overweight, with one-third more than 20 percent above their healthy weight.

Why does anorexia constitute a crisis? Data from the National Institute of Mental Health reports a mortality rate of roughly 5.5 percent per decade, which is about twelve times higher than the annual death rate due to *all* causes of death among females aged fifteen to twenty-four in the general population.[4]

The lives of these individuals revolve around food and weight concerns. Every bite of food, every calorie taken in and burned off, becomes the driving life focus. Fear of gaining weight is all-consuming. Refusing to eat is all about control. Early symptoms include depression, loneliness, helplessness, and hopelessness. Telltale symptoms include hair loss, cold hands and feet, fainting spells and compulsive, excessive exercise. Such exercise can be hidden. It is often done in the middle of the night and taken to the extreme. Anorexics will lie about their food intake, lie about the exercise, and often cover up the fainting spells and irregular heart rhythms that characterize a metabolism that's totally out of balance.

In addition, when the menstrual cycle fails because of significantly depressed estrogen levels, calcium is lost from the bone, just as in an aging woman. Key organs in the body shrink and lose functionality. Blood sugar and blood pressure often fall below normal levels, clearly a crisis of physical and emotional health.

---

4.   Ibid.

BULIMIA

Bulimia (*bulimia nervosa*) is an eating disorder characterized by binge eating (rapid and massive consumption of food at one sitting) followed by purging (induced vomiting, laxative abuse, diuretics). Some estimate that as many as 5 percent of college women are bulimic. Though they may not be severely underweight, this process of binging and purging leads to intense guilt and shame.

Those suffering from bulimia likewise have a preoccupation with body weight and shape. The purging can trigger depression and mood swings. Rather than being in control, they often feel out of control.

The forced vomiting can cause dental problems as well as throat and stomach issues. Heartburn, bloating, and swollen lymph glands can indicate bulimia. Once again, in young women menstrual cyclicity disappears because the nutritional status is poor. Dehydration can result, as well as permanent injury to the intestines, the liver, and the kidneys. Also, the imbalance in blood chemistry can lead to abnormal and potentially fatal cardiac rhythms. Obviously, eating disorders deserve prompt attention.

MINISTRY TO THOSE WITH EATING DISORDERS

Those suffering from eating disorders are fragile and vulnerable. Centers that specialize in treating such problems generally recommend inpatient therapy to redefine body image and reestablish normal nutrition and eating patterns. This is beyond the scope of the pastoral staff and ministry team unless the disorder is recognized very early. However, the spiritual input provided by the church ministry team can be instrumental in the process of recovery.

You should refer the person diagnosed with an eating disorder to a specialist in the field for inpatient treatment and strict behavior monitoring. Then you can join the individual and the family in long-term follow-up and follow-through that can lead to success. Restoring a proper sense of both body image and value in Christ—they must see themselves as beloved in the Lord—is essential.

It is not only naive but also genuinely harmful to tell someone suffering from anorexia or bulimia to "just stop!" Being told to eat right, exercise in moderation, and "quit all this foolishness" generally causes the sufferer to withdraw and become more secretive. As a result, the spiral continues toward death.

Ministry in this crisis will likely involve several layers of corrective thinking, including an understanding of the depth of the problem, reworking the wrong thinking that has led to the danger, and then rebuilding a healthy outlook and approach to life. This generally takes quite a long time and often involves setbacks. Prepare to love well over an extended period of time.

ADDITIONAL RESOURCES

Ayres, Desiree. *God Hunger: Breaking Addictions of Anorexia, Bulimia, and Compulsive Eating.* Lake Mary, FL: Creation House, 2006.

Mintle, Linda. *Breaking Free from Anorexia and Bulimia.* Lake Mary, FL: Strang Communications, 2002.

CANCER

It's the C-word. It strikes terror in the heart of anyone diagnosed with it—as well as those who love the person—but what exactly is cancer? *Cancer* is a general term for cells growing out of control. The normal cycle for human cells involves growth, maturity, multiplication, and cell death. Cancer describes cells continuing to grow without boundaries or control. Most cells in the body can grow in this fashion—so there are cancers of most types of tissue and organs (lungs, gastrointestinal tract, skin, and brain, to name only a few). Genetic factors or damage to cells from radiation, toxins, or carcinogens (e.g., tobacco, asbestos, alcohol) may cause normal types of cells to multiply out of control.

The specific cell type grows rapidly, eventually affecting the "host." These cells can either form a localized lump (tumor) or spread to distant parts of the body through the bloodstream or the lymphatic system (called metastasis). Different tumors spread different ways. Depending on its size and location, a tumor can be dangerous or fatal, even though "benign" in appearance. A tumor can invade nearby tissue structures or grow and exert pressure on nearby organs. Cancer can also metastasize when smaller groups of cells separate from the originating colony and move through the bloodstream to enter other organs or tissues located anywhere in the body.

Keep in mind that a diagnosis of cancer (tumors, lumps, lesions) does not equal death. Many live for years with cancer. When communicating with patients, doctors often use gentler, more vague terms because *cancer* has such a devastating impact. You should be aware that *lump, tumor,* and *mass* all mean a type of growth that does not belong, but these words offer no clues about whether the abnormal growth is cancerous, dangerous, or merely a nuisance.

Cancers are described not only by their cell type (pancreatic, lung, esophagus, etc.), but also by the "stage," which identifies how far the tumor has spread, and by the "grade," which describes how aggressively the cells are dividing. The higher the stage (1–4), the greater the spread; the higher the grade (1–4), the more aggressive the tumor. The objective of this descriptive system is to provide information about the prognosis and treatment plans. Interestingly, sometimes cancers that grow most rapidly are the most sensitive to chemotherapy. Their rapid growth enables some very effective treatment approaches. Grading is done by a pathologist, who examines the tissue from a biopsy (taking a piece of the tissue for microscopic study). This is important because cancers with more abnormal-appearing cells often tend to have a worse prognosis.

Even tumors that do not spread through the bloodstream or lymphatic system can be deadly. A growing tumor mass can block blood flow or press on vital structures, even though it's not spreading throughout the body. This process generally gives rise to recognizable symptoms. Whether or not a tumor can be safely and completely removed surgically depends upon its location.

Effective crisis ministry requires understanding these basics of the cancer diagnosis and treatment, and then utilizing the skills of hospital and home visitation (see chapter 3) to share God's grace and strengthen the afflicted.

CANCER TREATMENTS
Surgery

With surgery, the goal is to remove all, or as much as possible, of the cancerous tissue. Because it is sometimes impossible to be certain that all the tumor cells have been removed and not "spilled" during the operation itself, other therapies, called "adjunctive," may be appropriate. These might include chemotherapy and/or radiation therapy. Ministry during postoperative recovery can have a powerful impact on healing.

Chemotherapy

Chemotherapy is simply the use of drugs to treat cancer. These medications are cellular poisons and will destroy the fastest-growing cells. They travel through the bloodstream and can reach those cancer cells that have spread from the primary source. Cancer centers across the world correlate their research and statistics to develop the best protocols for various types of cancers. Chemotherapy has enormous and often predictable side effects. Caring for someone in the midst of cancer diagnosis, staging (the regions of spread of this cancer), and treatment will require patience and an understanding of how these tests and treatments may affect the body.

Anticipate that the fastest-growing normal cells in the body also will be affected. These include hair cells, blood cells, and cells lining the gastrointestinal tract, which explains the complete hair loss for many, the often-constant nausea, and the pervasive fatigue. Evidence that the chemotherapy is working may be a significant anemia and susceptibility to infection (from the decreased number of white cells, which are central to the body's immune system). Realize that the patient's fatigue is genuine (some medications are available now to combat this), and keep pastoral visits short. And, of course, avoid visiting if you are ill. What may be a minor cold/flu for you could be absolutely devastating to someone on chemotherapy.

Radiation

High-powered waves of energy, such as X-rays or gamma rays, are designed to target the cancerous cells in order to destroy them. Radiation can be targeted or can involve large sections of the body to try to eradicate any remaining tumor cells. Efforts are made to protect healthy surrounding tissues to minimize side effects. Radiation therapy also can involve the injection of radioactive materials that target specific cells (thyroid) or pellets and rods that can be used to locally destroy certain tissues. The effects of radiation treatment also often include fatigue and nausea, so keep visits short, respect the patient's energy level, and don't take it personally if some days the patient is simply too tired for a visit. Again, it isn't about you; it's all about sharing God's love for a brother or sister in need.

Immunotherapy

An understanding of how antibodies attack antigens has led to many new types of therapy. Trying to mark tumor cells with materials that the body's immune system will recognize and destroy has been an effective approach in treating some forms of cancer. This avenue of treatment will be expanding in the years to come. Side effects seem to be less than with chemotherapy or radiation therapy, and recovery may be faster.

COMPASSIONATE CARE AND COMFORT

Life with cancer brings constant adjustments and trials. Your compassionate presence and faithful prayer form the foundation for ministry in this crisis. Availability to help on the good days and the bad will make an impact on the person suffering with cancer as well as on the person's family.

- Listen well and patiently.
- Provide compassionate presence with soft eye contact and relaxed body language.
- Limit your time during hospital visits. A cancer patient has less energy than before the treatment began, so follow the fifteen-minute rule unless specifically asked to stay. Leave the children at home (unless they are the children of the patient!). Don't be intimidated by the monitors, wires, and tubes. Become familiar with these "tools of the medical trade" so you neither disturb them nor are troubled by them (see chapter 3).
- Be an encourager, and use humor with caution.
- Find out about any necessary chores, and do them or provide for them to be done.
- Remember the patient's spiritual need for prayer. Allow God to touch the heart as you offer a brief, tender prayer.

Cancer causes some people to feel distant from God or question their faith. It is important to comfort and appropriately encourage those who face a battle with cancer. Ministers and friends need to come alongside those who are hurting and point to God's faithfulness, sovereignty, and protection, recognizing that sometimes cancer may lead to death.

Despite seeing his city destroyed, Jeremiah speaks of God's faithfulness (Lam. 3:22–23). While God may permit His child to "go through the fire" of various trials, He never will leave or forsake that one. Ultimately, such testing may result in praise and glory to Jesus Christ (see 1 Peter 1:6–7). In 2 Corinthians 5, Paul looks to the hope of a new body after this old one passes away. Throughout Scripture we see that God demonstrates His faithfulness in every trial, including death.

The Psalms provide not only the hymnbook for the nation of Israel, but also the God-inspired words to put emotions and thoughts before the Lord for all God's people in every generation. The psalms of lament are the most prevalent forms of expression, teaching us how to cry out to God in times of despair. Examples of these are Psalms 6 and 13. Psalm 23 has comforted many with the promise of a safe future in the presence of God. It is important to know that there is no safer place than in God's protection. Psalm 4:8 speaks of the safety of being nestled in God's care.

Such verses certainly can bring comfort, but allow the Spirit to control the timing for sharing Scripture with patients undergoing therapy. Consider creating a list of verses that have been meaningful to you, and leave it with patients to read at their leisure, in private, when they feel like approaching the Lord.

Jesus has promised never to leave us or forsake us. We have confidence, even when we don't fully understand the plans of God, that His ways are far above our comprehension (Isa. 55:8–9). According to Romans 8:28, God does work all things together for good for His children, but this verse is best brought to mind by the Spirit of God rather than the minister applying it too soon. Treating the body requires accurate diagnosis and appropriate treatment at the most effective time. Likewise, for the soul in pain, the Word of God administered at the right time by the Spirit of God brings genuine comfort.

Not all suffering is ultimately bad, as God often uses it to transform individuals into Christlikeness and to draw observers to a deeper sense of God's glory. But this is His prerogative and His process. We must humbly allow God Himself to direct this journey.

Cancer can be "cured," though medical doctors generally speak in terms of five- or ten-year recurrence-free intervals. Life is never the same after cancer. The individual will wonder each day, with each new ache or pain, whether the cancer has returned. Thus, the task of ministry will be ongoing. Be patient. Recurrence often implies that the cancer has developed a resistance to chemotherapy and/or radiation. So the prognosis (future expectations) may be less favorable. Hearing that the cancer has returned can cause an overwhelming shock. And once again, the opportunities to minister through prayer and presence are paramount.

ADDITIONAL RESOURCES

American Cancer Society at www.cancer.org.

Babcock, Elise NeeDell. *When Life Becomes Precious.* New York: Bantam, 1997.

Jeremiah, David. *A Bend in the Road.* Nashville: Word, 2000.

Knox, Sally M., and Janet Kobobel Grant. *The Breast Cancer Care Book.* Grand Rapids: Zondervan, 2004.

National Cancer Institute at www.cancer.gov.

SUICIDE ASSESSMENT AND PREVENTION

People in difficult circumstances may at times find life useless, hopeless, and not worth living. With the fatigue of fighting terminal illness, deep depression, or fractured family relationships, suicide may seem to offer escape from the pain. With the knowledge that death brings one into the Lord's presence, believers who face serious physical or emotional pain may find suicide particularly attractive. Faulty thinking characterizes those in crisis, including seeing their problems as insurmountable. Such thinking may make alternatives difficult to conceptualize. Every aspect of life seems bad, and from their perspective each negative circumstance seems to be personally targeted at them. Everyone and everything appears to be stacked against them.

When dealing with a person who is potentially suicidal, you simply must *ask* direct questions. Since all people have value as persons, I will ask anyone with depressive symptoms if he is thinking of taking his own life. I also ask if he has begun to believe that his life is not worth living. I will intentionally ask the question several ways in an effort to get at the truth. Sometimes, the depth of the pain becomes apparent slowly in crisis situations, so you must be patient.

MYTHS ABOUT SUICIDE

Let us dispel some common myths about suicide:

- Asking about suicidal thoughts does not put ideas into people's heads! Most who have considered suicide consider it a great relief to be able to talk about it. Those who have not contemplated their own death will often smile and reassure you that things are not that bad. In either case, your task is to identify those whose pain is so deep that their lives may be at risk. Ask!

- People who talk about ending their lives *do* commit suicide. They are not just "looking for attention"; rather, they are probably crying for help.
- A person who has struggled with suicidal thoughts will not necessarily always be suicidal. People heal and crises end.
- Suicide is not an inherited trait. Though people who have seen and experienced suicide in their families are certainly at greater risk, there is no genetic impetus for them to take their lives.
- Suicidal people are not insane. They are often just overwhelmed with circumstances, sleep deprived, and depressed—making rational thought and sound decision making impossible. If sufficiently fatigued and sleep-deprived, any of us will experience profound depressive symptoms and the inability to concentrate well.
- Suicide is *not* the unpardonable sin. The sacrifice of Christ is sufficient for everyone who has genuinely trusted in Jesus.

When a person who was seriously considering suicide shows signs of improvement, has the danger passed? No! Often when a suicidal person has made the decision to end his or her life, a feeling of relief takes over, causing that person to behave much more "normally" until the moment that the person has determined to kill himself or herself arrives. So, be prepared to walk with this person until healthy habits have been fully restored.

Remember, in most (not all) cases of suicide, there are some warning signs. Remember too that suicide is not the end of all suffering. For the one who does not know Jesus, suicide seals that person's separation from God.

SUICIDE RISK ASSESSMENT

When working with a person whom you believe presents a risk of suicide, think in terms of a continuum of danger. How great a risk exists? Is the person in immediate danger? In your mind, develop a system of worrisome and encouraging signs to help you know when you need to refer the person for immediate help or hospitalization.

Factors that indicate high risk include 1) previous suicide attempts; 2) a detailed plan for committing suicide, including how, where, and when; and 3) lethality of the plan. A child who will "hold her breath until she dies," for example, is a low risk; someone who keeps a loaded gun at the bedside because it gives a reassuring sense of control is a very high risk. Hanging also has high lethality. Overdosing on pills falls in the middle, depending upon the drugs, whether mixed with others, and how many are taken. Most doctors prescribe potentially dangerous medications in amounts that will be unlikely to cause death. Suicidal patients, however, obtain medications from several doctors and may empty the medicine cabinet mixing all manner of drugs, producing a lethal effect. Drug overdose may signal a genuine cry for help, and there is often time to take the person to the emergency room and save his or her life.

Additional risks include a "familiarity" with suicide from other family members and prolonged physical or mental health problems, including psychiatric diagnoses or substance abuse. Anything that can cloud the thinking can increase the risk of a "successful" suicide attempt.

As you interview those at risk, pay attention to expressions of hopelessness, isolation, and/or abandonment. Statistically, older white males and men with financial or job-related problems are at greater risk. Women with relational fractures (divorce, abandonment by loved one) are at an increased risk.

Positive factors that can balance out the risk include solid social networks, friends, family, and people who love them. A person who is able to see different solutions and express hope in the midst of the crisis (so-called cognitive flexibility) is not at the highest risk. A person who retains hope and has not been battered by a succession of crises likewise will be at lesser risk for suicide.

During your interview, investigate the person's spiritual life, including church and worship involvement—even worldview—to find areas of strength and hope. How does the person relate to the pastoral staff? Does she feel supported, encouraged, or neglected? Is the person involved in areas of service that can give her a sense of God's grace and involvement in her life even in the midst of the crisis?

Always err on the side of safety. If you believe the person is at risk for suicide, get help.

Ultimately, you will make an assessment. Considering the high-risk predictors of suicide balanced against the protective factors, you must decide whether to continue the soul care yourself, to refer that person to a physician, or—if you sense a high enough danger level—to personally accompany the person to the local emergency room for evaluation. There have been rare occasions when I did not feel comfortable letting the person leave my presence. More often, a firm commitment that the person would not commit suicide and would call me if he or she felt overwhelmed prior to our next meeting would allow the process of healing to unfold. Depending on your comfort level with this particular crisis, you should be aware of local resources, hotlines, and other counseling support. Always err on the side of safety. If you believe the person is at risk for suicide, get help.

Simply put, you must decide whether to continue the counseling process yourself, refer the person to someone with more experience or training in this area, or arrange for hospitalization. This may take the form of inpatient therapy and then progress to outpatient therapy, regular consultation with a physician, or counselor care.

Ministry to the Family Following a Suicide

Depending upon the scope of your church ministry, eventually you will likely be called upon to minister to the family left behind by a suicide victim. Sometimes there is a note explaining the "reasoning," sometimes not. Occasionally the note gives insight into the factors precipitating the death, other times the outpouring of words just confuses and deepens the survivors' pain and guilt.

The normal grief of loss is compounded by the apparent senselessness and selfishness of the act. Expect a range of emotional response that may include anger, disappointment, even fear alongside the mourning process. Your presence communicates genuine care, but additionally a few theological thoughts can begin to comfort the surviving friends and family.

When Jesus speaks of the "unpardonable sin," He speaks of blasphemy against the Holy Spirit. Thus, suicide is not unforgivable. Suicide does involve the voluntary taking of a human life, and is therefore sin. However, one who has inherited eternal life is kept in the very hand of God and cannot be plucked out (John 10:28; see also John 3:16; 14:1–6; 2 Tim. 1:12; 1 John 5:13). The believer who commits suicide does not forfeit salvation because depression, despair, or life circumstances became more than they could handle.

Oftentimes friends and family assume the guilt for the suicide, believing they could have or should have done something to intervene. While competent counseling can often change the dynamic, by no means can all those contemplating suicide be identified and turned around. When listening to those sharing these guilt feelings, if you do identify these burdens, prayerfully offer grace and understanding. There are resources below to complement your ministry and enable the survivors to both grieve and find personal peace in the midst of this tragedy.

ADDITIONAL RESOURCES

Biebel, David B., and Suzanne L. Foster. *Finding Your Way After the Suicide of Someone You Love*. Grand Rapids: Zondervan, 2005.

Black, Jeffrey S. *Suicide: Understanding and Intervening*. Phillipsburg, NJ: P & R Publishing, 2003.

Carr, G. Lloyd, and Gwendolyn Carr. *Fierce Goodbye: Living in the Shadow of Suicide*. Scottdale, PA: Herald Press, 2004.

Cox, David, and Candy Arrington. *Aftershock: Help, Hope, and Healing in the Wake of Suicide*. Nashville: B & H, 2003.

Hsu, Albert. *Grieving a Suicide: A Loved One's Search for Comfort, Answers and Hope*. Downers Grove, IL: InterVarsity Press, 2002.

National Institute of Mental Health, Suicide Prevention at www.nimh .nih.gov/suicideprevention/index.cfm.

Suicide.org at www.suicide.org.

Townsend, Loren L., and Daniel G. Bagby. *Suicide: Pastoral Responses*. Nashville: Abingdon Press, 2006.

END-OF-LIFE ISSUES

Unless the Lord returns first, we will all experience death at some point. We are aware of this reality throughout our lives, yet we humans shy away from the topic of death and dying because it often brings a sense of fear, as we anticipate much that is unknown.

Scripture on Death and Dying

The Bible has much to say about death, dying, and the significance of each life. As we consider the end of the earthly, temporal existence, familiarize yourself with the texts below, allowing them to frame your thinking. Contemplating death can be both frightening and mysterious. Our God who fashioned us inspired several scriptural passages that have brought comfort over the centuries and have been the focus of many funeral messages. Think through the implications of this collection of scriptural passages as you minister during life, through death, and in anticipation of life everlasting.

> A psalm of David. The Lord is my shepherd, I lack nothing. He takes me to lush pastures, he leads me to refreshing water. He restores my strength. He leads me down the right paths for the sake of his reputation. Even when I must walk through the darkest valley, I fear no danger, for you are with me; your rod and your staff reassure me. You prepare a feast before me in plain sight of my enemies. You refresh my head with oil; my cup is completely full. Surely your goodness and faithfulness will pursue

me all my days, and I will live in the LORD's house for the rest of my life. (Ps. 23)

Do not let your hearts be distressed. You believe in God; believe also in me. There are many dwelling places in my Father's house. Otherwise, I would have told you, because I am going away to make ready a place for you. And if I go and make ready a place for you, I will come again and take you to be with me, so that where I am you may be too. (John 14:1–3)

Now this is what I am saying, brothers and sisters: Flesh and blood cannot inherit the kingdom of God, nor does the perishable inherit the imperishable. Listen, I will tell you a mystery: We will not all sleep, but we will all be changed—in a moment, in the blinking of an eye, at the last trumpet. For the trumpet will sound, and the dead will be raised imperishable, and we will be changed. For this perishable body must put on the imperishable, and this mortal body must put on immortality. Now when this perishable puts on the imperishable, and this mortal puts on immortality, then the saying that is written will happen, "Death has been swallowed up in victory." "Where, O death, is your victory? Where, O death, is your sting?" The sting of death is sin, and the power of sin is the law. (1 Cor. 15:50–56)

For we know that if our earthly house, the tent we live in, is dismantled, we have a building from God, a house not built by human hands, that is eternal in the heavens. For in this earthly house we groan, because we desire to put on our heavenly dwelling, if indeed, after we have put on our heavenly house, we will not be found naked. For we groan while we are in this tent, since we are weighed down, because we do not want to be unclothed, but clothed, so that what is mortal may be swallowed up by life. Now the one who prepared us for this very purpose is God, who gave us the Spirit as a down payment. Therefore we are always full of courage, and we know that as long as we are alive here on earth we are absent from the Lord—for we live by faith, not by sight. Thus we are full of courage and would prefer to be away from the body and at home with the Lord. So then whether we are alive or away, we make it our ambition to please him. For we must all appear before the judgment seat of Christ, so that each one may be paid back according to what he has done while in the body, whether good or evil. (2 Cor. 5:1–10)

For to me, living is Christ and dying is gain. (Phil. 1:21)

Therefore, if you have been raised with Christ, keep seeking the things above, where Christ is, seated at the right hand of God. Keep thinking about things above, not things on the earth, for you have died and your life is hidden with Christ in God. (Col. 3:1–3)

Now we do not want you to be uninformed, brothers and sisters, about those who are asleep, so that you will not grieve like the rest who have no hope. For if we believe that Jesus died and rose again, so also we believe that God will bring with him those who have fallen asleep as Christians. For we tell you this by the word of the Lord, that we who are alive, who are left until the coming of the Lord, will surely not go ahead of those who have fallen asleep. For the Lord himself will come down from heaven with a shout of command, with the voice of the archangel, and with the trumpet of God, and the dead in Christ will rise first. Then we who are alive, who are left, will be suddenly caught up together with them in the clouds to meet the Lord in the air. And so we will always be with the Lord. Therefore encourage one another with these words. (1 Thess. 4:13–18)

And I heard a loud voice from the throne saying: "Look!
The residence of God is among human beings. He will
live among them, and they will be his people, and God
himself will be with them. He will wipe away every tear
from their eyes, and death will not exist any more—or
mourning, or crying, or pain, for the former things have
ceased to exist." (Rev. 21:3–4)

As Christians we know death is a transition from this life into the
presence of our Lord for all who trust in Him. For those who have
rejected the gospel, death means eternal separation from God. To those
who are believers, we can speak comfort and peace. With those who are
dying and have not trusted in Christ, we have the sacred privilege of
sharing the gospel that saves souls.

How does one die? What does death look like? You likely have attended
funerals and know what death looks like after the mortician has prepared the deceased for viewing. People these days react negatively
to death in its raw reality, so with proper lighting and makeup, the
deceased can be viewed and remembered well.

Some of us have attended those sacred moments when the spark
of life departs, the soul leaves the body, and the shell, the "seed" of
1 Corinthians 15, remains. Death is not natural. It was not part of God's
plan for the first family, Adam and Eve. Sin caused death to become a
part of our reality. The expulsion of Adam and Eve from the garden of
Eden prevented their partaking of the Tree of Life, so they ultimately
died physically, having already experienced spiritual death, or separation from God. But death is a defeated foe according to Scripture, and in
God's gracious plan, death prepared the way for a physical resurrection
to a new kind of life, an eternal life with sin fully and forever atoned for.

END-OF-LIFE DECISION MAKING

Biblically, death means separation. Physical death means separation
of the soul from the body, and spiritual death means separation of the
soul from God. In fact, the believer has already "died" to sin and is hidden with Christ in God (Col. 3:3). There is no need for the believer to
fear death, for the Christian's soul is secure for all eternity.

From a medical standpoint, physical death can be hard to define. In days past, the cessation of heartbeat and breathing was used to determine point of death (clinical death). Yet with cardiac bypass machines, people can live for hours during a surgical procedure without a beating heart (and without a heart at all during a transplant operation!) while "breathing" by way of oxygen supplied to the blood by a machine. Now we generally think in terms of brain waves as determinative of life, but lower brain activity (not thinking and feeling, but the signals that initiate respiratory effort) may persist for some time after clinical death. These distinctions become very important when speaking of "brain death," persistent vegetative state (PVS), and suitability for organ transplant. In order to transplant organs upon the "death" of an individual, the organs must be perfused with blood and oxygen to keep them usable. Many have adopted the definition of death as when the living tissue fails to function as a "coordinated organism." Blood cells are alive, but they are not a life. Fingernails and hair continue to live and grow for some time after death is declared, but the *person* is no longer living.

As we move to consider decision making at the apparent last stages of life, we must consider the complexity of such issues. Your insight and input as a minister will be requested. Questions about breathing machines, do-not-resuscitate (DNR) orders, and feeding tubes for comatose or "brain dead" individuals will test your ability to prayerfully think through these issues and speak truth with kindness.

Crisis ministry as death approaches often will involve more than your godly presence; it will involve help and direction in thinking through the complicated decisions that accompany the end of life. With incredible advances in medical science, people are living longer. Many diseases that used to be fatal are now responding to therapy. Yet ultimately, for each person, the hour of death will come.

Medicine can substitute for and support many organ systems for a time. Ventilators help with oxygen. Dialysis handles kidney function. Cardiopulmonary bypass

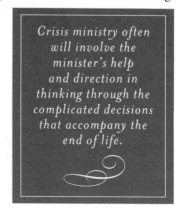

Crisis ministry often will involve the minister's help and direction in thinking through the complicated decisions that accompany the end of life.

supports the circulation. And parenteral nutrition (tube or IV feeding) handles food requirements. But nothing of this nature lasts forever.

When is it time to say "enough" and to turn off the life-support systems? Is it ever appropriate to refuse certain treatments? Most people would like to live to be one hundred years old, die peacefully in their sleep, and leave a godly legacy of both Christian character and treasure behind. However, life doesn't often end that way.

In years past doctors often refrained from telling patients of impending death for fear of upsetting them. And physicians hesitated to prescribe sufficient pain medicine, concerned that patients might develop addictions. But today there is a medical specialty in palliative care (i.e., not curative, but keeping the patient comfortable), and the best long-term research demonstrates that it is best for patients to know the seriousness of their condition so they can "get their house in order" and prepare to meet the Lord. It borders on the ludicrous to be concerned about developing an addiction when someone is nearing death. Many people are more afraid of the pain involved in dying than of death itself. For most patients, pain relief can be successfully achieved, putting to rest this overriding fear of dying "badly."

For the minister, end-of-life moments require some courage and ability to engage graciously in difficult circumstances. Hopefully, a relationship is already established, so a level of trust exists between you and the dying person. Be willing to talk about death and the life after death. Be concrete with your words, not vague, and speak the truth in love. It is especially important to become familiar with the terminology used in hospital settings so that you can understand and help translate the recommendations that are being made. There are two terms in particular you need to grasp.

- **Aggressive Therapy.** Aggressive therapy is doing "everything possible," using all available methods of sustaining life, including ventilators and full resuscitation efforts. This will virtually always be the approach until a firm diagnosis is established. For example, if a young person is involved in a serious motor vehicle accident and arrives at the emergency room unconscious, he or she will require "aggressive therapy," including all the technologies available. Immediately after such an accident, it's impossible to assess the extent of the injuries, the possibility of brain damage, and the probability of return to consciousness and function. Anticipate this if you enter someone's crisis in the emergency room and decisions are being made.

• **Euthanasia.** In other situations, discussion might involve *euthanasia*, which comes from the Greek word meaning "good death." While most would want a "good death," this term is used for willfully and directly causing that death. While not legal in the United States, it is an accepted practice in some countries, like the Netherlands. The definition is refined as "voluntary euthanasia," where the patient requests a lethal injection or method; "involuntary euthanasia," where the patient has refused to be euthanized; or "nonvoluntary euthanasia," where the patient has neither requested nor refused euthanasia. Some include "withdrawal of treatment" in this category. This involves terminating or withholding life support, allowing the patient to die. Finally, "indirect euthanasia" (sometimes called accidental or inadvertent euthanasia) involves giving a medication to help the patient, but the unwanted side effect causes death (for example, narcotics suppress the drive to breathe, so it is possible when trying to relieve a patient's pain with narcotics to cause the patient to stop breathing).

Ethicists from various religious and nonreligious perspectives have written extensively on this bioethical crisis. My perspective in this manual sees euthanasia, the willful taking of a human life, as wrong, as sin. Euthanasia violates the sanctity of human life and is an affront to the image of God in humanity. However, in my opinion, withdrawal of treatment, deciding not to initiate an aggressive course of therapy, or stopping a ventilator when no realistic hope of regaining consciousness exists may at times be ethical and appropriate.

One ethical system within a Christian worldview concludes that it is never right to do wrong. God didn't call us to make history unfold in our preferred way but rather to walk in obedience. Thus, we should find the will of God, via Scripture and prayer, as we address each problem individually. Knowing what God's Word says, are we then able and willing to do it?

End-of-life decisions are among the most difficult crises people must face. Pastors, deacons, and other servants of Christ often become part of the "family circle" when these circumstances arise. How do we prayerfully and thoughtfully discern the mind of the Lord when a loved one approaches death and further medical intervention seems futile? The decision paradigm I share here comes from the Biobasics Series, to which I contributed.[1]

When faced with a life-threatening event and considering treatment options, the status of the patient's consciousness is primary. If the patient is awake, alert, and an adult, he or she would be most helpful in making these decisions. If, however, the patient is comatose, decisions will need to be made by others. Ordinarily, there is no rush to decide, so this decision-making scheme comes into play only after appropriate diagnostic testing has been completed and results are available. From this point on, our discussion will concern the person who is unconscious or unable to make his or her own decisions.

It is essential to know whether the condition is reversible or irreversible. If the condition is reversible (curable), measures should be undertaken to maximize the opportunity of recovery. Often one cannot accurately predict, however, whether certain conditions, heart problems, and/or cancers would be reversed by heroic measures.

Should the condition be deemed irreversible, comfort care (palliative therapies) should be initiated. This "worst case scenario" of an unconscious person with an irreversible condition will arise in your ministry at some point. Commonly called "persistent vegetative state," these people have settled into an apparently irreversible, unconscious state.

It's worth mentioning here that people are *never* and should *never* be considered vegetables. *Vegetative* means alive but without cognitive responses to external stimulation. Even in this most dire of circumstances, every person is worthy of dignity and respect for every person is made in the image of God. So "care" is never withdrawn. We always

---

1.   John Kilner and Gary P. Stewart, eds., *Basic Questions on End of Life Decisions*, Biobasics Series (Grand Rapids: Kregel, 1998).

care for people. However, aggressive, heroic medical measures may not always be appropriate or required.

Alert, competent patients can and should make such decisions for themselves. Ideally, each individual should plan ahead and give the gift of his or her thought processes to loved ones. Consider the various end-of-life directives such as a living will and/or a durable power of attorney for health care. These documents, which must be available to family and physicians, will allow the individual's wishes to be known and will help the caregiving team to honor those wishes. The living will allows the individual to outline the procedures that he or she would prefer or would reject in certain circumstances. This helps loved ones avoid the dilemma and conflict of when to say "enough." The weakness is that every possibility cannot be anticipated. The durable power of attorney for health care designates another specified individual to make end-of-life decisions in the event that the individual cannot make them for him- or herself.

Many Christians agree that individual patients should not be forced to undergo experimental therapy—or even heroic resuscitation efforts—if there is no genuine hope for a cure. For example, to resuscitate a patient with end-stage metastatic cancer just so he or she can die again shortly thereafter seems both futile and unkind. Concern arises with questions surrounding feeding tubes and hydration for the comatose person. Does this mirror "giving food to the hungry and drink to the thirsty brother in need" that Jesus equated with ministry to Himself (Matt. 25:34–40), or an invasion of personal autonomy? As a physician and pastor, my sense is that when a patient cannot take nutrition in an irreversible comatose state, intervention with feeding tubes or central lines does represent "aggressive medical therapy." Not every patient must have such intervention, though the decision should be made in the light of all the facts unique to that case. Recognize that as death approaches, the "nonessential" bodily functions tend to shut down, including the gastrointestinal tract. Thus, "force-feeding" a dying person might actually increase the person's discomfort and offer no real benefit.

Every opportunity to minister in these end-of-life situations requires prayerful, individual consideration. There are often neither easy nor obvious answers as to how to proceed. The sanctity of each human life, the condition of the particular individual, and the stated wishes of the patient all play a part in helping the patient and the patient's family as decisions to treat or withhold treatment become necessary.

ADDITIONAL RESOURCES

Focus on the Family. *Caring for Aging Loved Ones.* Wheaton, IL: Tyndale, 2002.
Rae, Scott, and Paul Cox. *Bioethics.* Grand Rapids: Eerdmans, 1999.
Smith, Wesley. *Forced Exit.* New York: Times Books, 1997.

PART 3

PREVENTIVE
MEASURES TO
AVOID CRISIS

PREMARITAL COUNSELING

One must look all the way back to Genesis and the creation of man and woman to gain foundational insight into the nature of marriage, since the institution of marriage hinges on God's *intention* for the relationship between man and woman. The roots of that relationship are anchored in the concept of mankind, made in the image of God.

> Then God said, "Let us make humankind in our image, after our likeness, so they may rule over the fish of the sea and the birds of the air, over the cattle, and over all the earth, and over all the creatures that move on the earth." God created humankind in his own image, in the image of God he created them, male and female he created them. (Gen. 1:26–27)

Although modern theories of the image of God are varied, the relational aspect of this concept is prominently expressed in the above verses. Just as God exists in relationship within the Trinity (as indicated by "let *us*" and "after our"), so God created man to exist in relationship first with God and also with other human beings. In the relationships with other humans, the male-female relationship deserves special attention.

In the second chapter of Genesis, this idea of relationship is further developed following the description of woman's creation from the man's rib, as indicated by the admonition that "a man shall leave his father and his mother and hold fast to his wife, and they shall become one flesh" (Gen. 2:24 ᴇsv). This "holding fast" as translated in the English Standard Version, or "uniting" as indicated in the New International Version, carries the implications of a unique relationship between the man and the wife. The verse implies that the man and the woman both have left their homes by virtue of the new relationship, reflecting a particular pledge of commitment to one another.

The design of human anatomy provides for a physical union of man and woman that literally results in the joining of the two who have been symbolically united by the marriage pledge. The idea of the durability of this union was emphasized by Jesus when He declared, "Therefore what God has joined together, let no one separate" (Matt. 19:6). Thus, a marriage that fails fractures a covenantal agreement. A biblical covenant such as this represents a promise or vow with God as witness and participant. To ward off the ever-growing possibility of divorce among Christian couples, marriage should be entered into thoughtfully, prayerfully, and with eyes wide open to the significance of the relationship and God's intentions for its durability.

THE MARRIAGE RELATIONSHIP PYRAMID

Premarital counseling that focuses on developing genuine intimacy in marriage can provide a vital step in getting a marriage off to a good start. The diagram represents the three key aspects of the marriage relationship, showing that a healthy, godly marriage emerges from a foundation of spiritual intimacy. Other aspects of marital life, while  important, are dependent upon a deepening relationship with God, which draws husbands and wives closer together over the years.

The starting point within a Christian marriage is spiritual intimacy. From the moment the couple says "I do" until the Lord calls one or both of them home, they are "spiritually one." That doesn't mean they share one spirit but that God has declared a new, unique union that exists to bring glory to Himself.

Although God saw that what He made was "very good" after the woman was created (Gen. 1:31), all was changed after the fall and the expulsion from the garden of Eden. Thus the core problem each couple must recognize involves the fallen condition of every individual, which leads to self-indulgence, self-reliance, and self-centeredness. Salvation does not eliminate these fleshly tendencies. To overcome them, the Christian couple needs to rely on the empowerment of the Holy Spirit.

A biblical understanding of the parameters for marriage is also essential. These are found in Ephesians 5:21–33, 1 Peter 3, and even Philippians 2, where we see Jesus Christ "empty" Himself for others. Applying Ephesians 4:32, "Be kind to one another, compassionate, forgiving one another, just as God in Christ also forgave you," can be foundational to relational maturity. The couple must be prepared to grow up in Christ, learning to treasure one another, trust one another, talk with respect and understanding, and learn to face trials together. Additionally, premarital counseling should emphasize that the three primary stressors of a marriage are time issues, money problems, and gender distinctions—each of which can be a blessing that unites rather than a problem to overcome.

Another component of the pyramid is relational intimacy. Allow me to define intimacy as "being fully known and deeply loved, without fear of rejection." Clearly, at the spiritual level, only God can love us this way perfectly. Yet as a couple grows together and toward Christ, a deeper experience of this type of intimacy should be realized.

Threats to intimacy to be considered before marriage include sexual exploitation while one was growing up, unconfessed sexual sin, and unexpected stress (financial, medical, relational, etc.). Premarital and marital counseling can and should address these issues. Marriage may be a one-flesh union, but that union is not to be regarded as purely sexual; rather, marriage is a collaboration, simultaneously a work of art and a work in progress. It's a work of art in that no two marriages look exactly the same. It's a work in progress because transformation occurs over a lifetime together. So we can expect change and delight in the process as the seasons of life unfold.

The final level of the intimacy pyramid, and the smallest in terms of time spent over a lifetime, regards physical intimacy. Sexual intimacy constitutes an important part of marriage, but it's not the only part or even the most important. God has designed man and woman to unite in a way that can bring great delight to the couple. For physical intimacy to be experienced fully, however, spiritual and relational intimacy also must flourish. Thus the three-tiered picture of intimacy represents God's overall plan for the married couple.

THE BIBLICAL PORTRAIT OF MARRIAGE

Whereas the biblical source of marriage can be seen in the creation, the biblical portrait of a marriage can be viewed in the following verses. Every person who feels led to counsel in this vital area of Christian life should be very familiar with these passages:

- Sacrificial love (Eph. 5:21–23)
- Submissive love (1 Cor. 7:3–5)
- Self-surrender (Gen. 2:24)
- Physical support (1 Tim. 5:8)
- Emotional support (1 Peter 3:1–7)

To understand what Ephesians 5 so beautifully pictures, one must study this passage in context (as always!). The thematic structure of the book can be seen in the exhortations to "walk": to walk worthy, to walk in light, to walk in love, and to walk in wisdom. The details of that wisdom include not being "drunk with wine" but being "filled by the Spirit." In fact, the discussion on wives submitting to their own husband as to the Lord and husbands loving their wives as Christ loved the church picture what a Spirit-filled married life looks like.

Submission by a wife is not a role but an expression of spiritual maturity, which leads to *voluntary* acts whereby she works alongside her husband. She willingly sets aside her rights to the glory of God and for the sake of the growth in godliness of her husband. You can force obedience but not submission. True biblical submission is a decision of the will that evidences Spirit-filled maturity. The wife should lend cooperation, imagination, and implementation to her husband's endeavors. Submission is not being a doormat or a silent partner. Her role is not one of inferiority, and she does not have to tolerate or enable abuse. In addition to submission, the passage concludes with a directive for a wife to respect/reverence her husband. This is unconditional. She is to respect the position of husband. He does not have to earn respect (just as he is to love her, and she does not have to "earn" his love). This always requires the supernatural enabling of the Holy Spirit!

For the husband, his love for his wife is not conditional either. The imperative to the husbands likewise is impossible without the enabling of the Holy Spirit. Husbands must love as Christ loved. Thus, a godly husband displays sacrificial love (laying down his life; not just being willing to, but actually putting his wife above himself), sanctifying love (encouraging her growth in godliness), and satisfying love (physical pleasuring as part of the covenant). By modeling the love pictured in 1 Corinthians 13, a godly husband is patient, kind, not jealous, and not keeping account of wrongs or rejoicing in unrighteousness. He demonstrates a love that never fails. He submits first to the Lord but also exhibits mutual submission within the body of Christ ("Submit to one another out of reverence for Christ," Eph. 5:21). Part of the beauty of Ephesians 5 portrays the husband/wife unity using head/body imagery. The husband's wife represents part of his own body, with Scripture declaring the husband as "head." Thus, God has endowed the role of husband with derivative authority. He faithfully *follows* Jesus, his head, while the wife *follows* him. Christ is the head of the home. Thus the Christian husband is called to a sacrificial love whereby he loves his wife and honors her "as a fellow heir of the grace of life, so that nothing will hinder his prayers" (see 1 Peter 3:7). The counselor must be alert to determine if the couple is ready for their individual callings as husband and wife in regard to godly, selfless love.

QUESTIONS FOR THE COUPLE CONSIDERING MARRIAGE

- Have both of you trusted Christ's ultimate sacrifice to reconcile you to God?
- Do you long to be like Jesus? To follow Him?
- Are you both heading in the same direction with shared goals?
- Do others who know you well have a positive assessment of your relationship?

- Do you really want to marry this person? Why?
- Are you marrying each other "just as you are" or are you depending on major changes to take place in your spouse-to-be and/or your relationship?

Other areas for productive discussion include:

- Commitment to a local church
- Financial responsibilities
- Division of duties: household chores, keeping the checkbook, cooking, etc.
- Children issues: How many? How soon? How will they be educated?
- Family-building issues (use or nonuse of contraception)

As premarital sessions unfold, look for areas of inflexibility, blind spots, or merely topics that the couple has not yet considered. I recommend meeting with a couple four to six times prior to the wedding ceremony. I use my book *Sexual Intimacy in Marriage*, but other fine resources are also available. Individual answers to questions are not as important as how the two communicate. Respect, love, and grace are essential in their interactions, and a sense of humor doesn't hurt!

My personal conviction is not to preside over a wedding ceremony where either party is an unbeliever. If there is doubt in your mind, prayerfully present the gospel along with your convictions about marriage as God intended it.

ADDITIONAL RESOURCES

Akin, Daniel. *God on Sex*. Nashville: B & H, 2003.

Boehi, David, Brent Nelson, Jeff Schulte, Lloyd Shadrach, and Dennis Rainey, editor. *Preparing for Marriage*. Ventura, CA: Regal, 1997.

Cutrer, William, and Sandra Glahn. *Sexual Intimacy in Marriage*. Grand Rapids: Kregel, 2007.

Eggerichs, Emmerson. *Love and Respect*. Nashville: Integrity, 2005.

Kostenberger, Andreas. *God, Marriage, and Family*. Wheaton, IL: Crossway, 2004.

Rainey, Dennis, and Barbara Rainey. *Starting Your Marriage Right: What You Need to Know in the Early Years to Make It Last a Lifetime.* Nashville: Thomas Nelson, 2007

Thomas, Gary. *Sacred Marriage.* Grand Rapids: Zondervan, 2002.

CHILD PROTECTION POLICY

In ministry to children, especially, preventive measures can be taken to avoid major crises. Churches must provide a safe, secure, wholesome environment for the spiritual growth and development of children and youth. We sadly live in a time where abuse of children, even within the church setting, is escalating rapidly. Young people lack the ability to recognize and escape potential threats, so we must be intentional about each program, every worker, and all the situations surrounding children in the church.

Consider your current church policies for hiring staff and using volunteers in children's ministries. Below is a sample policy adapted from the one used by Shively Baptist Church in Louisville, Kentucky. Various churches have such policies, and you can likely access many of them via church Web sites. Whatever your approach, you should have thoughtfully and prayerfully prepared to select those individuals who will be entrusted with the care of the precious children of your congregation.

POLICY FOR MINISTRY WITH MINORS

This policy is intended to assist [church name] in screening and training all volunteers and staff who work with minors. We also want to operate within the guidelines of this policy and plan for any circumstance that might arise.

Recruiting and Selecting Workers

1. You must be a member of [church name] for at least one year before being considered to work in the nursery, preschool, children's, or youth departments.

2. All workers must complete an application and background check. All references will be checked. Applications will be viewed only by ministerial staff and then secured in a safety box.

3. All new applicants must be interviewed. Current workers may be interviewed. All interviews will be conducted by ministerial staff.

4. Workers will view *Reducing the Risk of Child Sexual Abuse in Your Church*. This video will be shown periodically during the year by ministerial staff. Further training and information will be made available.

Supervision

1. All classroom doors for ages eighteen and younger will contain windows or else the doors will be left open while the classrooms are in use.

2. A minimum of two workers shall be present for *all* scheduled activities.

3. Any preschool, children, or youth activities, excluding regularly scheduled meetings, shall be approved by the church staff and placed on the church calendar.

4. The ministerial staff or a designee shall randomly monitor activities of the various classrooms.

5. Church staff and volunteer workers will obtain the consent of any minor's parent or guardian before going out alone with the minor or spending time alone with the minor in an unsupervised situation. The workers will also notify an appropriate minister of such meetings in advance.

Reporting Allegations

1. Any claim of inappropriate behavior shall be reported to a ministerial staff member immediately.

2. To protect both the alleged victim and the alleged offender, the following steps will be taken:

LANCE WYSE
Church Design Consultant

DESIGN BUILD+

737 South Third Street
Louisville, KY 40202
O: 502.992.5105
f: 502.992.5101
lwyse@lfdesignbuild.com
www.lfdesignbuild.com

...sion ▪ Plan ▪ Design ▪ Construct

• A written statement or transcript will be taken by the ...

... nts or legal guardian of the alleged victim will ...ed.

... ised will be notified.

... ts in responding to the allegations will be doc-... l and confidential to help protect individual's ... gainst false accusations.

... he church's attorney or a ministerial staff mem-... senior pastor shall interview the parties involved ... ke appropriate recommendations.

... required by law, a report of the allegations will ... e to the appropriate authorities and the insurance ... ny.

... iterview regarding the incident can occur before ... xt scheduled activity, a designated person shall ... he activity.

... nterviewing the parties involved, the investigating persons will prepare a preliminary statement of their findings. This will document adherence to the church policy and provide information and conclusions for the pastoral leadership to consider. Care should be taken with this document as any legal proceedings will access this information.

• At the conclusion of the investigation, appropriate action will be taken.

Records: Background Check

Records of an applicant may be checked through any or all of the following:

• Child Abuse Neglect (CAN) Central Registry Check
• Kroll Background America

Other checks as deemed necessary may be performed.

ADDITIONAL RESOURCE

Sample Policy and Procedures Manual: Child Abuse Prevention and Safety Policy; www.baptist.ca/acrobat/guides/child_safety_sample _manual.pdf.

CHURCH DISCIPLINE

Some of the crises you will face not only involve an individual but also affect the entire church. Such issues as domestic violence, marital infidelity, and other sexual sin may require a response that ministers to both the person involved and the body of believers.

THE BIBLICAL PROCESS

When the crisis arises from personal sin, particularly unrepentant sin, the church leadership has an obligation to deal biblically with the situation. Fortunately, the process is rather clearly outlined by Jesus, as recorded in Matthew 18:15–17 (emphasis added).

> If your brother sins, go and show him his fault when the two of you are alone. If he listens to you, you have regained your brother. But if he does not listen, take one or two others with you, so that *at the testimony of two or three witnesses every matter may be established.* If he refuses to listen to them, tell it to the church. If he refuses to listen to the church, treat him like a Gentile or a tax collector.

Jesus describes a situation when a "brother"—a believer—commits a sin against another believer. To summarize, the response involves:

- *Private communication.* The offended person goes to the offender and tries to solve the problem face-to-face. Should genuine repentance and confession take place, restoration is full, and the process is concluded. The goal is restoration of the sinning individual and the return of harmony and unity within the body.

- *Plurality of confrontation.* If the offending individual fails to respond and seek restoration, the offended person returns with one or two additional spiritually mature people. They all hear the case and prayerfully encourage resolution of the conflict, as well as restoration of the unity fractured by the offense. If the offender repents, the process ends, and God is glorified.
- *Public declaration.* If the offending individual refuses to respond favorably to the offended and the other witnesses, the case will be presented to the church. One last time the offender has the opportunity to repent and resolve the offense. At this point the weight of the prayers of the entire church body is brought upon the situation so that the unity in the Spirit might be restored.
- *Exclusion from church fellowship.* If the offending individual refuses to respond to the clear, loving confrontation of the church, the individual is excluded and considered an unbeliever. This represents a serious step of discipline. Exclusion from the spiritual hedge of protection that the church provides has serious ramifications for the soul. The offender has acted consistently like an unbeliever and is to be considered as such. As with any unbeliever, the individual can attend services and hear the gospel, but should be excluded from the celebration of the Lord's Table. Hopefully the individual will experience genuine conversion and then seek restoration with the offended person.

This is a slow, methodical process. One should never embark on exercising church discipline without having prayed sufficiently over the matter to be genuinely broken and humbled over one's own sin. When your desire is to go and confront "this wretched sinner," your heart is not rightly prepared to undertake such a sacred task. Remember that at every step, restoration is the goal. Christ outlined church discipline and entrusted this ministry to the church for the health and unity of the body. Prepare yourself prayerfully so you do not enter this arena of spiritual warfare ill equipped.

WHEN A CHURCH LEADER FALLS

How does the church handle a staff member or leader involved in sexual, financial, or other sin? The question always arises whether or not such a one should be dismissed from leadership or whether forgiveness of the offense includes full restoration to church office. Assuming the leader is fully repentant, here are a few guiding principles I have found helpful in the practicalities of church ministry:

- Confession of sin should extend at least as far as the knowledge of the sin.
- For a church leader, the responsibility of the position often requires such confession to extend to the church body in order to stifle gossip that would dishonor the name of the Lord.
- Some offenses disqualify an individual from church leadership positions, at least for a time. The qualification for a pastor/elder to be "above reproach" does not require sinless perfection but does imply a life of integrity, humility, and honor. Certain sins may damage the reputation and character such that it may take years to restore; and certain sins may do irrevocable damage. The Levitical priests of the Old Testament times were disqualified *for life* from service in the temple should they sever a finger or part of a finger in their ministrations over the sacrifices. Some sins may disqualify one permanently, not from service, but from certain offices.

Proper exercise of church discipline honors God and purifies the church body. All who are members of the local congregation entrust themselves to the leadership under God. Failure to practice church discipline leads to dysfunction within the church and damage to the spread of the gospel. Church membership is a sacred privilege, as we submit to biblical authority and correction and strive together to walk worthy of the calling of Christ.

ADDITIONAL RESOURCES

Dever, Mark. *What Is a Healthy Church?* Wheaton, IL: Crossway, 2007.

Dever, Mark, and Paul Alexander. *The Deliberate Church.* Wheaton, IL: Crossway, 2005.

Mosgofian, Peter, and George Ohschlager. *Sexual Misconduct in Counseling and Ministry.* Dallas: Word Publishing, 1995.

Whitney, Donald. *Spiritual Disciplines for the Christian Life.* Colorado Springs: Navpress, 1994.

Appendix

Case Studies

These case studies are designed for group discussion. The cases presented are actual stories or blended accounts of similar stories. They are designed to help the person desiring to minister to think through real-life crises and develop broad, practical strategies for the various scenarios.

In my years in medical practice and in the pastorate, I have heard some remarkably insensitive things said by well-meaning people. As has often been said, no situation is so bad that a little guilt can't make it worse! Some people simply can't abide silence and feel they must say something, even if it is inappropriate. So I include a sampling of these insensitive responses with each case study in order to stir conversation. While you may have thought some of these things, I hope you learn not to speak them audibly! Following the case studies, I comment on each scenario.

CASE 1: SUDDEN DEATH

Rachel, a forty-five-year-old, active church member, driving home in her own car behind her daughter in another vehicle, sees her daughter's car hit by another automobile. The daughter's car bursts into flames, and Rachel watches her child die. Nine months after the services, Rachel continues to watch the video of the funeral almost every night. She has not changed a thing in her daughter's room and visits it reverently every day. At times she says she sees her daughter, and she often hears her and responds to her. These "conversations" bring her comfort. She often dreams of her daughter, healthy and whole.

Her husband asks you to come and talk with her. How do you prepare for this conversation? Should you or someone else have been visiting regularly in the intervening months?

Insensitive Responses

- "Change the room, give away all the daughter's clothing, and don't let Rachel watch the video anymore. It's morbid!"
- "It's been long enough. She needs to get out and get involved!"
- "She's just crazy. She'll never get over it."

CASE 2: POSTPARTUM

Nita, a twenty-five-year-old mother of a two-week-old infant, refuses to leave her room. She won't come out to eat, and she doesn't want to hold her baby, see her husband, or have any visitors. She refuses to get out of bed, shower, dress, or do anything. She doesn't want to live.

You are invited to come by for the normal "pastoral visit," having not noticed anything unusual during the hospital stay. You arrive to find an exhausted, exasperated husband, and a wife who doesn't want to see you or anyone from the church. How do you respond?

Insensitive Responses

- "You have a beautiful baby and wonderful husband! Snap out of it!"
- "You probably aren't a very good mother."
- "Lots of women get the 'blues' after a new baby. You'll be fine! Just get up and do something!"

CASE 3: RELAX!

Wes, a twenty-four-year-old male student, comes to the emergency room with chest pain and numb fingers and hands. He can't catch his breath and fears he is going to die. His young wife accompanies him, equally petrified. She has called you, the pastor/deacon/Bible study leader, because they know and trust you. When you arrive at the ER, they are being prepared for discharge. The doctors "found nothing wrong, gave him a pill, and told him to go home and relax."

How would you respond?

Insensitive Responses

- "I want to talk to the doctor right now! They don't know what they are doing around here!"
- "Relax? You got a case of the nerves! I drove down here for nothing!"
- "I know someone they told that to just last month, and he died!"

CASE 4: POSTABORTIVE

Carla, an eighteen-year-old deacon's daughter, tells her parents she's pregnant. The guy she's been seeing wants to "do the right thing," but he is an unbeliever, immature in every way. Her father calls their pastor, who arrives and suggests that the best thing in this situation would be to terminate the pregnancy and put this matter behind them. Desiring to save face and protect the family name, her parents concur, and she has an abortion.

Now, four years later, she comes to your church to talk to you about her decision and about the feelings she's been experiencing. She has symptoms of anxiety and depression and disillusionment with the church and its leaders, and she wonders where God was in her crisis. How do you respond?

Insensitive Responses

- "No good Christian has an abortion! That's unthinkable!"
- "Your symptoms are God's punishment for killing your baby."
- "What kind of pastor would ever advise you that way? You must have misunderstood."
- If you counsel or comfort her, she won't learn her lesson.

CASE 5: INFERTILITY

Tricia has been trying to get pregnant for years. She and her husband have spent thousands of dollars for medical testing and treatment. So far, several miscarriages are the only results. They struggle with how far they can go ethically and how much they can spend as good stewards. Their friends and family are growing weary of the ongoing moodiness and "obsession" with all things fertile.

The couple calls you for advice and counsel. How do you respond?

Insensitive Responses

- "If you'd only adopt, you'd get pregnant! I knew a woman who adopted, and six months later, bam! She was pregnant!"
- "God opens and closes the womb, so just pray and trust God."
- "You don't know how lucky you are not to have kids! You and your husband have so much freedom to do whatever you want."
- "Want kids? Borrow mine!"
- "Just can't get it right? I'll send my husband over to tell yours how it's done. He just looks at me and I'm pregnant!"

CASE 6: PREGNANCY LOSS

Paula was twelve weeks along in her pregnancy when an ultrasound at the doctor's office revealed that the baby had died. The doctor recommended a dilation and curettage (D&C) within the next day or two. Paula is distraught, and her husband has no idea how to comfort her. Together they had desperately wanted a child. All their friends and family knew about the pregnancy.

Paula has her husband call you. How will you respond?

Insensitive Responses

- "I know just how you feel. Our cat died last week."
- "There was probably something wrong with the baby anyway."
- "Well, at least you know you can get pregnant. I'm sure it'll go fine next time."
- "I knew a woman whose doctor said the baby was dead, but he was wrong! You should get a second opinion."

CASE 7: PORNOGRAPHY

Troy, a twenty-five-year-old seminary student and part-time youth pastor, is discovered to be looking at online pornographic sites using the church computer. You become aware when computer upgrading reveals this to be an ongoing problem. When you confront him, he at first denies it; but when the evidence is presented, he confesses, insists it isn't really a problem for him, and promises he won't do it again.

How will you proceed? What are your obligations to your brother in Christ? Will you inform his wife? What, when, and how much will you tell the church regarding the situation?

Insensitive Responses
- "He's a young, healthy male. Those sites aren't the bad ones."
- "Now that he's confessed and asked forgiveness, shouldn't we forgive him and move ahead? After all, he is really growing the youth group."
- "We don't want to destroy his marriage or his future ministry. Let's just handle it quietly."

CASE 8: DOMESTIC VIOLENCE

You are notified by one of your church members that she has taken out a protective order against her husband and is planning to file for divorce. Her husband, a regular attender for more than twenty years, has a reputation for anger issues. When you visit the wife, you notice bruises and bandages, and you discover that she was seen in the emergency room, again, for injuries resulting from physical violence against her, allegedly by her husband. How will you respond?

Insensitive Responses
- "If my husband ever hit me, I'd shoot him in the head."
- "What did you do to make him so angry?"
- "You can't file for divorce—he hasn't been unfaithful."
- "Why have you stayed with him this long?"

CASE 9: CANCER

Forty-five-year-old Lucy, a pastor's wife, is diagnosed with cancer during a routine screening test. After the pastor notifies the rest of the church staff, he asks for some privacy while decisions about treatment possibilities are made.

How do you minister to your pastor, his wife, and his family when such a crisis arises?

Insensitive Responses

- (To the pastor, from the deacons) "Church members are pretty mad that you said you don't want any calls or visits now."
- (To the wife) "I hope you don't die."
- (To the wife after chemotherapy causes total hair loss and requires a wig) "I never liked your hair the way you wore it anyway."
- "I know exactly how you feel. I knew someone who had cancer and . . ."

CASE 10: DNR

Caleb, a sixty-year-old gentleman, was hospitalized for a severe flu-like illness. The disease progressed rapidly, rendering him comatose. Diagnostic tests as yet are inconclusive, but he is not responding to powerful antibiotic and supportive therapy. The doctors are requesting a do-not-resuscitate (DNR) order.

The family has requested to speak with you. What will you recommend? How will you think through the process of decision making at life's end?

Insensitive Responses

- "He'll be better off."
- "You need to let him go. Just trust God."
- "They've done all they could. It's in God's hands now."
- "He wouldn't want to live as a vegetable."

ADDITIONAL HISTORY AND SUGGESTIONS ON THE CASE STUDIES

Case 1: Sudden Death

A tragedy of this nature can overwhelm anyone. Seeing your child consumed in flames is almost beyond the imagination. This case was as profound a grief as I have ever encountered. The "enshrinement" of the daughter's room is worrisome, though grieving to a year or more would still be normal. Is she functioning in other areas of her life, or has she withdrawn? Dreaming about a lost loved one is quite normal; hallucinating, along with seeing and conversing with the loved one, is not. Most people have a "sense" of the loved one's presence, or feel like they "caught a glimpse" of him or her, but genuine hallucinations require immediate attention. Most people just need an echo for their grief, a loving companion to walk through this valley with them. On occasion medical help is beneficial, particularly in circumstances of severe sleep deprivation (which will lead to depression and other symptoms) or the abnormal grief described in this case.

Case 2: Postpartum

The "baby blues"—symptoms of depression following the birth of a child—are very common (happening to close to 80% of moms). However, these symptoms virtually always resolve by two weeks after the birth. The 10 to 15 percent of women having symptoms that last longer than two weeks have postpartum depression, a serious and significant mood disorder that not only causes disruption in the household but also can be dangerous for the new mother. These women genuinely feel miserable and they cannot, by themselves, "snap out of it." Quality research has demonstrated significant help with medications until the hormonal cycles return to normal. Remember that the enormous hormonal swing from pregnant to nonpregnant can overwhelm some women, and with every pregnancy they face an increased risk of this depression.

Understand the severity of true postpartum depression (less than 1% go on to postpartum psychosis, involving hallucinations, homicidal, and/or suicidal thoughts, etc.). Get her some help! She needs medical consultation, help with the baby, and help for the husband and the rest of the family. Church families often cover meals and so forth for the first couple weeks, but after all the other help has gone home, the new moms can feel desperate.

Case 3: Relax!

Panic attacks are very scary! Even young, healthy people believe that they are dying. The fear triggers hyperventilation (hence the numbness) and the tightness in the chest really does hurt. Other possible diagnoses involve genuine heart disease, lung issues, and gastrointestinal disorders. If the exam and laboratory tests were normal and the patient responded quickly to the rhythmic slow breathing and/or anti-anxiety medications, discharge pending any return of symptoms makes good sense medically. Try to help the patient not feel foolish or that he is overreacting. Reinforce the good news that there doesn't seem to be a major medical problem, and pray for rest and calm in the Lord. These crises can be infrequent or episodic, and some have identifiable stress triggers.

Case 4: Postabortive

In my opinion, based on years of experience in crisis pregnancy centers, postabortion syndrome truly exists and causes considerable emotional pain. Sometimes the physical consequences of abortion are primary, but most often, some years after the procedure, the reality and horror set in. This presents the minister with an incredible opportunity to minister grace. Listen to the story prayerfully, and provide support. Encourage the woman to take responsibility for the decision, to accept the loss, and to grieve the loss.

Case 5: Infertility

This case involves infertility and the ethics of assisted reproductive technology. If you encounter such a crisis-counseling situation (more than one in six couples suffer from infertility), you will need careful theological reflection. I suggest *The Infertility Companion*, which I coauthored with Sandra Glahn (2005) to help pastors, counselors, and patients cope with the many stresses and difficult issues involved in infertility diagnosis and treatment. Before you oppose any procedures, have the curiosity and integrity to investigate precisely the procedures being considered. Are there ethical issues involved? Is the sanctity of human life at risk in a particular procedure? What are the financial ramifications of each decision? I believe Christian couples can prayerfully think through the ethical maze of fertility workups and treatments. Having a child is a good goal, for a child truly is a gift from God. Encourage the couple to pursue appropriate means to try to arrive at that goal.

Case 6: Pregnancy Loss

First trimester miscarriage (spontaneous abortion) happens frequently, so you will no doubt encounter such a situation. Early signs include cramping and bleeding, but with early ultrasound, accurate diagnosis can be made quite early. Generally speaking, a baby who dies prior to six weeks gestation can be passed by the mother without surgery. At more than twelve weeks, the mother almost always requires D&C to avoid major prolonged bleeding and risk of infection. Some judgment is required between seven and twelve weeks.

For many couples, having a few days to process and grieve prepares them for the finality of the miscarriage. You can help in such a situation with an ongoing supportive presence, recognizing that this is indeed a profound loss. A tiny human who will never again experience life in this temporal sphere has died. The comfort comes, though, in the realization that each life does have eternal significance, no matter how long one lives.

Clarify your theological understanding of human death in utero so that you can minister effectively. I believe such tiny souls are taken to God's presence. I have total faith that the God of this universe does right.

Husbands and wives grieve differently. Assure them that this difference is normal. Grief is processed over time, and should they conceive again, there is heightened anxiety until the gestational age of death is passed with the next pregnancy. Be sensitive, be patient, and be present as needed. Help with the notification calls so others won't make insensitive remarks unintentionally.

Case 7: Pornography

Christians are to live lives worthy of Christ, pursuing holiness in all things. Clearly, exposure to material that generates sinful desires, causing lust for persons or objects that cannot be rightfully satisfied, constitutes sin. In this case the immorality involves a staff member, a man called to lead and to model and to live "above reproach." His spiritual health takes first priority; thus, confrontation by mature leaders will be necessary.

Once genuine repentance and confession takes place, forgiveness can be freely received from the Lord. However, forgiveness does not necessarily restore this man to the qualifications necessary to hold his position of leadership. The pastor and other staff will need to prayerfully evaluate the specifics of the case. In this example, the sin was ongoing, long-standing, and initially denied. Healing from this type of dangerous compulsive behavior will likely require ongoing accountability. Most would immediately remove him from his leadership responsibilities and work to preserve and strengthen a marriage that may be totally based on falsehood. Sensitivity will be required here, as well as informing the church why such action was taken against a staff member.

While I would hesitate to recommend a detailed listing of the sins and sites involved, it would be appropriate to inform the church, perhaps in the Wednesday night setting, that moral failure was involved. Being too general may leave the congregation open to gossip about adultery or other forms of failure, so sufficient detail might be appropriate (i.e., moral failure related to inappropriate use of the Internet). Depending upon the maturity level of the youth leader caught in this sin, he could make a personal confession to his assembled youth group with pastoral leadership present, or the pastoral leadership could read a written confession, composed by the youth minister. In any case, ministry to the disillusioned youth, and their parents will likely become necessary.

Case 8: Domestic Violence

The statistics about domestic violence are deeply disturbing. We often ask the wrong question. It shouldn't be "Why does she stay?" but rather

"Why does he hit her?" Such physical abuse is clearly sin, and the church has an obligation to address that sin with the goal of restoring the abuser and healing the marriage. Statistics would suggest that such a resolution is rare. The battered wife (and children, if present) deserves protection. Personal safety in these instances is a priority. While the church leaders sort out the issues, a safe environment should be provided for the wife and children. This is a "separation for safety," not a legal separation or a preparation for divorce. Scripture doesn't mention domestic violence as a justification for divorce, but it outlines clearly the process of church discipline that leads either to restoration, or treating the unrepentant offender as an unbeliever (see chapter 18).

Case 9: Cancer

When cancer (or other serious medical diagnosis) hits a church staff member, it always upsets the rhythm of the church's life. People who genuinely love the pastor and his wife desire to help in meaningful ways, even if the couple desires some privacy to work through the issues. Remembering that the focus of crisis care should be on the person in crisis, the wife and her husband should be permitted and encouraged to communicate what sort of help they need, both immediately, and as time and treatment unfold. Being well intentioned does not excuse making a difficult situation worse.

The pastor can communicate to the congregation the needs and appropriate updates so that the congregation feels "connected" and involved. Usually, the time soon comes when all sorts of tangible expressions of help and support become valuable and appreciated. We tend to want to "rush to the rescue" rather than being willing to fight the good fight over the long haul. Cards that express concern and prayers are always a good idea until more tangible expressions become necessary.

Case 10: DNR

This end-of-life case actually involved my father. While the doctors were trying to get my mother to sign the DNR order (which she would have done, thinking Dad did not want to live on a "breathing machine"), my father had a cardiac arrest. Since the forms weren't yet signed, the doctors did a full resuscitative effort. They got him back to a normal rhythm and discovered from a pending lab test that he had a deep bone infection, requiring higher doses of a fairly routine antibiotic. He fully recovered and lived a productive ten years more. The lesson here is that there is no need to hurry signing a DNR order! However, there may well come a time when medical capabilities are exhausted and no reasonable outcome can be expected from resuscitation.

Try to get the medical facts as known and the best prognosis envisioned. Prayerfully work with the family through the patient's wishes, including their feelings in response to the medical information. Each case is unique. Breathing machines and feeding tubes are quite useful in someone who has a reversible condition or one who has life expectancy with some level of mental clarity. Such interventions are not "required" but are available by the grace of God through medical science.